W9-ADZ-732

Karma & Sexuality

KARMA & SEXUALITY

The Transforming Energies
of Spiritual development

ZULMA REYO

Ashgrove Publishing
London & Bath

CONTENTS

CONTENTS

PREFACE

Many of the examples in this book have been drawn from the case histories of my clients and friends, and the observation of the variants in different cultures. I have included as many varieties of relationship as possible, centred around the primary experience between members of opposite sex. Parents and children, brothers and sisters, and other blood relations, as well as the many expressions of friendship (and enmity) may draw their own insights from the material presented.

The contents of this book may shock some people and perhaps disturb others who may prefer to point the finger rather than face the deep inconsistencies and untruths upon which normal relationships are built. In living with my own problems and limitations I have come to understand and value the experience of those imperfections in me which have allowed me to come closer to another human being.

The depth of my own human experience has also allowed me to appreciate the difference and equality of the sexes, and the tremendous possibilities that open up when two persons blend in the purifying fire-light of the heart. This meeting releases considerably more benefits when the sexual relationship is understood, allowed to unfold, and raised to embody the Father-Mother totality of the Creator. This journey is outlined in the last chapter. It is the most arduous, the most perilous and also the most glorious of all human experiences.

From peaks of reactiveness to extremes of graceful surrender, the course of life unfolds. To all our relationships, past and future, we owe the realization of ourself.

INTRODUCTION

Being real is not as easy as we think. It can't be commanded and it doesn't happen instantly. It requires that we take a deep and serious look at the way we relate to the world, to our relationships (all of them!), and our values. It is a complicated art of retraining perception, changing paradigms, and looking beyond duality upon ourselves.

This book is the second in a series of teachings known as Inner Alchemy. Mastery: The Path of Inner Alchemy, my first book, describes the basic philosophy of Inner Alchemy founded on two basic tenets:

(1) At the centre of each living form, including living tissue, the individual personality, and the soul, there is a point of light which represents the seed of God within every part of His creation. Nothing can exist without this inner life. Enlightenment, unity, health and harmony are only possible in as much as they reflect their attunement to Source.

(2) This basic pattern repeats itself in various simultaneous dimensions of human experience, replete with corresponding powers, faculties, 'bodies' and frequencies of expression.

Alchemy is the art-science of transmuting the lesser into the higher. This refers to physical substance over which we have dominion and responsibility. Inner Alchemy is the practice of Human Alchemy, the transmutation of our own world or the evolving of inferior material creation into its higher correlate and the expansion of consciousness or intelligence. This naturally reflects upon the physical body, the personality, personal surroundings and the general environment of the individual, his family and his world.

This present book gives us a clearer understanding of Inner Alchemy as it applies to the human alchemical experience. This experience is gained through relationships – the way a human being grows and develops that which is known as consciousness. Three concepts are introduced which make this clear:

(1) The theory of sub-personalities coexisting within the cellular human structure of personality as it expresses itself in three ways – physically, emotionally and mentally. This understanding allows us to marry the apparently contradictory impulses of matter and spirit through the knowledge of cause and effect, attraction or repulsion. It also helps us develop compassion and understanding which pave the way towards peace and better human relations.

(2) The dynamic between concentric and linear force which underlies the function of consciousness in matter. This blends the notion of human and divine into a single experience. We come to understand how mind and physical-material phenomena interact in our own selves. Two different atomic principles outlined in modern nuclear physics are in operation in our world. These reflect our kinds of relationships and mirror our prevailing values manifesting as conflict and tension, or as harmonious syntony.

(3) The theory of the redemption of matter is seen as a personal dynamic which reverberates upon planetary evolution. Responsibility is viewed as a personal experience of love and fulfilment.

The expressions of the personality are examined here in the human alchemical experience as a relationship dynamic. I chose to describe the energetic components of behaviour, in their esoteric as well as psychological and physical aspects, as clearly as possible, so that whoever wishes to gain that real autonomy which leads to discernment can consider the principles. I also hope to have sorted out the prevailing confusion regarding relationships of different sorts. Here they are examined within a single operational framework. Normal everyday relating, friendship and romantic involvement express differences of quality and degree. In essence they involve the same dynamic: the interchange of vital, bio-physical energies, the circulation of these in circuits which transcend physical space, and the sharing of lessons or experiences which can only be obtained by the reflection of another living soul.

This is not an ordinary book about relationships. It is an in-depth study of chakra psychology and the energy dynamics of spiritual evolution between brothers and sisters who express godliness through two distinct polarities: God Himself as masculine leadership and God Herself as feminine receptivity. The first five chapters of this book outline the energetic anatomy of the human personality, while also delineating the essential ingredients which constitute the spiritualization process, or the building of consciousness. Here the concept of sexuality as vitality is explored, laying bare the mechanisms operating among persons of the same or opposing gender in all the different relationships.

Our sometimes anguished, at other times exhilarating experiences in relationship compose stages of growth through different kinds of unfolding. As the energies of the elements, and with them the counterpart psychology dive deeply within, weaving through subterranean passages of need, pain, fear, and confusion bordering on madness, they emerge again and again renewed. Each time we may discover ourself as a new and richer human being.

Zulma Reyo

Infinite Absolute Being!
With the boundless light of the son
and your tenderness as mother…

Guide as ever on the way
Towards greater love
And understanding
Of your laws
And the gifts which we have
Your children, have
Upon this sacred Mother Earth

And…
May we ever feel
Your protection on the journey home,
As we fall and rise again
Into that greater glory
Which 'I am' in you

Amen

For now we see through a glass darkly
But then face to face. Now I know in part;
But then shall I know even as I am known.

(Corinthians 13:12, King James Version)

Chapter One

HUMANITY AND THE INDIVIDUAL

In my earlier book Mastery: The Path of Inner Alchemy, I describe the human energetic anatomy and define the human being as a constantly unfolding creator. To wish, to desire, to think... doing or inhibiting... man aspires. In aspiring he is creating a blueprint of that which he desires. That blueprint absorbs the energy of the creator whether it becomes a tangible physical expression or not. We are cluttered with such thoughtforms that constantly influence and deform the perception of what is real.

That which feeds thoughtforms is essentially bio-physical energy. It is through the electromagnetic quality of these energy-forms that we determine our financial situation, our professional success, our social standing and our relationships. That which we attract or repel (or cause-effect) comes under the term karma[1] (see page 175 for notes to text), otherwise known as fate, destiny, or as some like to call it, luck.

Whatever is created in physical matter or quasi-physical substance is subject to the law of physics. This means that it must be eventually dissolved, absorbed or transformed. This is a natural condition. But the human being has free will and there is no obligation to ethically deal with our creations other than to bear the voice of our conscience. Karma conveys the idea that one reaps what one sows. But karma is more than that. It represents the sum total of deeds (creations) done, or not done by an individual within a given lifespan. It is his baggage as a record of activity. Encoded also in the psycho-genetical structure of individuals, it is passed on to the offspring. It feeds cellular memory.

An individual naturally learns to manage his powers and materials (i.e. energies and substance) by trial and error. Hopefully he learns to protect life. As his sensitivity deepens, his awareness attunes with natural ethics and biological laws. As life moves in rhythms, what is affected will effect the affecting agent in like manner because both agent and thing are linked by the one energy.

Concentricity and Linearity

Life unfolds in concentric webs of free-flowing and non-directional reality where we find ourself as both creator and creation. Within us these primordial creative forces manifest as bio-physical[2] energy which taps into, amplifies and reproduces source-energy. These forces reflect the ever-active Primal Matrix out of which all creation spins. All opposites, polarities, dimensions and realities exist simultaneously in orgasmic perpetuity.

Our anxiety today stems from the mistaken belief that through our intellect, which expresses itself in three-dimensional linear terminology and modality, we can control the Primal Matrix at multi-dimensional frequencies and realities which are beyond grasp. Hence madness and chance (the expression of natural law) are a continual source of frustration. Yet, enlightened or superior man partakes humbly of this matrix, knowing that IT (not him) is the true creative centre. He blends the skills of a disciplined organism, composed of body, mind and feeling to the creative energy, in much the same way that a good horseman merges with his prime horse. It is the horse's strength and power coupled with the compassionate intelligence of the master that produce feats of prowess and beauty beyond the capacity of either. Let us remember this as we relate to the worlds within and around us.

In order to administer bio-physical energies properly we must train ourselves and look upon all of creation with a humbled heart. Until we can do that, our creations will be the measly measure of an egotistical, pompously eluded little self. Let us consider the power of life that flows through us as God's power - the chaotic gorge of the Primal Matrix. Let us consider effects (the manifestation of the circumstances in our lives and relationships) as the result of the cycles of nature and of what we ourselves have planted here and now, without seeking to blame or praise God or life for it.

Man is the weaver and the unraveller of creations. Whatever appears beautiful, whatever appears ugly is his own reflection. Whatever is black, or white, big or small, strange, familiar or unknown... all bears the pulsing of the One heart of Creation.

Whereas man's physical power derives from his material body, his heart is the seat of the Living God, the wisdom which is love. In consciousness, concentric force and linear activity blossom to weave the dance of existence. Evolution depends upon the coordinated conscious expression of bio-physical energy and the wisdom of the heart.

The basic mechanism of life is the interplay of ying-yang, male-female, active-receptive, and concentric-linear forces which sets the foundation for existence and serves as man's raw materials. 'Interplay' draws from the meaning of the word 'play' as understood in the East. Sanskrit scriptures affirm that divine activity is 'leela'. Participation within 'leela' implies a measure of both activity and receptivity within a reality that is both linear and concentric simultaneously; in other words the right quantity of horsepower and human compassionate understanding, to use the earlier analogy. It is both a happening and a doing at the same time. It is focused, purified intentionality. Now the will of God has become man's will, not in blind surrender but in conscious yielding and cooperation. Just as the horse needs our intelligent direction and we need its power, so does the evolutionary process engendered by the Primal Matrix need our individuation and we need its life force.

Our natural bio-physical energy generates the raw power which compels self-expanding activity which is in essence neutral. It produces movement and as such our gender (sexuality) offers us lessons in the use of energy. Depending upon how we use the energy and what type of movement we produce, we grow or evolve in consciousness or we regress within the involutionary path. It is up to us to use it properly and attain to full consciousness. Full consciousness implies the expansion of energy transformed into faculty or ability, and also soul substance. In other words transmuted matter and force. Consciousness develops through form. This is why it is said that God needs our hands to touch with, to manifest Himself/Herself. We equate God with only perfected creation when in reality God is the whole or absolute including unmanifested potentiality.

Occultism recognizes two entirely different kinds of darkness: the one pertaining to the unmanifest womb of creation which contains within it the seed of light, or life, the other related to the darkness engendered by the human being himself, which is a wilfull negation of the light-life. The first is the Primal Matrix. The second is the creation of the black magician who specializes in personalistic, separatistic ideologies to forge power. The first draws from real power through connecting with the real centre. The second usurps power through abject manipulation and deviation of bio-physical energies from the life-source of living things. It is important to understand the difference between the two paths trod by humanity. Both involve the use of power.

It is not by whim that celibacy had been advocated in many religious and occult schools. Unenlightened, raw bio-physical energy, besides dissipating essential energy, can be dangerous for the unprepared and uninformed. Intending to protect and/or manipulate mankind, the sexual taboos imposed upon humanity handed over more power to authorities who came to control the masses by inflicting guilt and a sense of sin. Those who dared defy the taboos, in the greater part stressed self-gratification, carnal pleasure and the general misuse of bio-physical energy. Our life-power became the domain of dark forces.

Physical stimulation is pleasurable. In our ignorance however, we grant ourself licence to cultivate it by any means that enhance its pleasure-producing qualities. This kind of selfish thinking leads to greater indulgence in multiple forms of promiscuity. Worse, this kind of thinking leads to a perverted use of power which gets chanelled psychologically and artistically, causing the decline of culture and civilization.

Directly or indirectly during the process we call human life, vitality is a central issue. The roots of vitality as sexuality are inexorably linked to the source of organic life and life-creating activity. Humans partake of the bio-physical energy of animals with a great difference. The human element dictates the development of consciousness. This is predicated upon intelligent use of our animal resources and is intimately related to discernment.

It is almost impossible today to find sexually active persons who are pure. The extent of psychological pollution is overwhelming. Whether we engage in sex or abstain from it, we are not exempt from the onslaught of pornographic, guilt-ridden thoughtforms that infest our very life force. The evolution of our species and the ascension of humanity as a whole depends upon the right understanding and practice of sexuality.

When linked to the force of purity and light, which is synonymous with humility and respect, pleasure, while including physicality far transcends it to become not only an expression of light but a light-producing mechanism that causes cellular transmutation and regeneration. This kind of activity raises consciousness. Every time someone's consciousness is raised, the whole of humanity feels it, much as a cell becoming luminous illumines the entire organism. For we are in fact but a cell within the body of humanity.

In its origins, Tantra (which includes the occult science of utilizing sexual energies to attain enlightenment) was a practice designed to raise the level of consciousness of humanity by preparing pure and vibrationally elevated vehicles for life. A soul attunes itself to a physical vibration commeasurate with its need for experience. The prospective parents represent such frequencies. The quality of the energy results from the level of consciousness of the participants, not from the physical intensity of the experience.

Expansion of consciousness results when matter is transmuted into light. Transmutation is the expansion (at nuclear levels) of the atomic light-seed at the core of every form, including living tissue. This is the much guarded secret of alchemy.

The dynamic of transmutation can best be understood through the following analogy: Consider a human being as a whole (a circle). His essence as a seed, contains his potentiality as human consciousness (a dot at the centre of the circle). The created identity as personality is a small cubicle formation on the periphery. This little house represents all the characteristics which have been inherited and which constitute the physical, mental and emotional nature, arranged in a special way by the sum of experiences which the individual person has had. In other words, the raw material lent to the individual by the parents' genes goes into determining his inclinations, but the particular experiences the individual has lived, and the way (consciousness) in which he has used the material (by remodelling adapting or enlarging) determine his personality (the cubicle). In this particular map the kinds of material appear as layers around the periphery.

This personality, built around a genuine individuality as well as its egoism, also has a source point. It is this centre which allows the person to strengthen and refine his instruments. However, the centre of human consciousness (or the 'atman'[3]), is a point of light within the Primal Matrix (circle). It has no real form: it is pure poten-tiality. Form is an expression of three-dimensional time and space, a fruit of the light seed necessary to evolve a working model of the whole. Such is the function of the personality. It serves as a laboratory for the building of consciousness as it continu-ously selects and excludes different possibilities of being.

Drawing from the experience in matter (codified as DNA/RNA genetic factors) and from the centre as Human life force or intelligence, the personality defines itself as by a name, a particular nationality, profession, distinct likes and dislikes... accumulated throughout a lifetime. If expressive, this personality is said to be strong. If, on the other hand, the personality is consistently undefined, it is considered weak. If it is the kind of structure where influences in the way of discrepant subpersonalities, traits and obsessions occasionally leak through, such a character structure is considered eccentric. The so-called insane and also our common neurotic, who simply cannot control the personality from the vantage point of his limited artificially-created nucleus, fit into this latter category.

When the structure is rigid, the individual represses disparate instincts by force of will, accentuating his disconnection from the whole. When the structure is unde-fined, the individual avails himself of a wavering, evasive personality which lacks real power or force in the world. The neurotic, however, is aware of his turmoil. He senses the tremendous pressure of different forces within him. He finds himself divided and misunderstood.

What are these forces from the subconscious? Where do they come from? Some people have sought explanation for them in the repressive or lax conditions of the times, and whereas these do influence and mould the personality, the causes for this disturbance do not stem from external factors only.

CONCENTRIC MAP OF THE CONSCIOUSNESS-EXPANDING PROCESS:

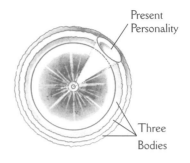

Present
Personality

Basic personality structure including the individual genetic ingredients at the level of all three bodies: the inherited equipment.
Father/Mother Principle: the unit of space within which the Primal Matrix containing the light seed exists. The monadic unit containing the potential causal body as well as the focus of consciousness.

Three
Bodies

Autonomous sub-personalitites, influences which exert a call upon the personality for resolution. Each unit, including the current personality-in-formation, contains a replica of the light seed. Each is covered by crystallizations (karmic adherences) which are separatistic influences corresponding to non-integrated tendencies.

The unconscious personality becomes a conscious vehicle for redeemed substance from the integrated units, representing new behaviour patterns. As each unit is absorbed, its imprisoned energy is released for expansion by the real centre, thus augmenting energetic capacity at cellular and personality levels, and strengthening the flow of consciousness between the centre and the now-conscious personality.

The expanded personality now includes the encoded information, abilities and energies from the sub-personalities to the proportion in which each has been assimilated.

There are no more unresolved issues. All matter at the level of the three vehicles has been transmuted. This represents an individual human expression of diversity and flexibility, the realization of life´s purpose. Consciousness as transmuted substance and force has achieved individuation and release from karma.

Within the individual bioenergetic complex and neuro-cellular structure are encoded autonomous energetic units of consciousness which are unfinished individuation processes bequeathed to us through the genetic structure of our ancestors. Each one of these also possesses an identity. They are actually incompleted personalities in the sense that they did not achieve individuation (Jungian term) or liberation (Buddhist term). They seek to complete their expression through the living blood and tissue of human experience and will not cease until this is achieved. In this way we can see how our ancestors truly clamour inside us, and how the work finished by one person liberates all those encapsulated energy units of those who went before him.

All living form seeks the plenitude of expression as completed or integrated consciousness, before it can find a higher expression. Herein lies the secret to understanding how the creations of humanity, the thoughtforms and impulses of negative individuals as well, must await a redirectioning by the light within human intelligence, coercing and influencing human experience until they are. All living things, in order to 'come to light', must be embraced by the light of consciousness. Transmutation is a process whereby a quantum of energy is incorporated and integrated by human experience. Until this can happen, that quantum of energy continues not only to act upon the grosser strata of astral dimensions, but it grows in force (is energized) through contact with human agents (who possess the living light seed) creating more alienation, and the darkness which opposes the very process of truth.

As a test case for the whole of humanity a human being offers a hope of redemption for incompleted lives crystallized by humanity before him. The personality struc-

ture offers an opportunity for them to become resolved. Only a human mind in a living form can contain, express, or transmute these quanta of energy.

We need to consciously transform and absorb inconsistencies into our personality
structure, making ourself flexible in such a way as to raise the whole. Such a process
is a prerequisite along the spiritual path. It is immensely important that each of us
face the reality of the subconscious (which often also includes the vein of many tal-
ents and unusual abilities). We must do so with a flexible and humbled personality.
In this process, the personality corresponds to the construction of character. The
personality structure must be strong, clearly defined and open. A weak structure
cannot possibly tolerate the intense influx from sub-personalities as they seek to
become absorbed within it. We must work on integrating our vehicles and transforming our energies. Through each part integrated we gain more and more energy,
power and momentum. When we are able to integrate all of our abilities, instincts
and tendencies we might say that we achieve full liberation or individuation and are
able to access the capabilities of the whole.

In our concentric map the Christ Self is the light-seed that expands progressively
with every successful absorbtion achieved at the three-dimensional level. Each time
that we absorb and transmute one of the sub-personalities, its energy passes on to us
as light-force, augmenting our vibrational field and our degree of dominion over
matter. As time goes by, and with successive transmutations, our light centre grows
to such magnitude that we are able to incorporate the frequencies of the causal
body. At this point, however, it is not us as an ego identity but as a focus of trans-
egoic consciousness. Acting through the integrated vehicle of the three bodies we
may now express a unit representative of Humankind. Such is the process of individuation as defined by occult science.

An individuated person is liberated from subconscious or karmic pressure. At this
point a causal body is built, or as I describe in my earlier work, the lower self
becomes one with the Christ Self. The focus of consciousness overtakes the entire
monadic (or human prototype) form. A Master is born.*

The expanding process of life and the alchemical linear map that I used in my first
book are included here. The difference lies in whether the individual defines a
source outside himself in order to link up with essential quanta of energy or force, or
whether he decodes the sourcing within himself directly. One might say that the linear map appeals to devotional temperaments whereas the concentric or circular map
serves the more holistic frame of mind.

* See also illustration No.2 - pgs18/19, and No.3, p20.

LINEAR ALCHEMICAL ALIGNMENT 1A

Father/Mother Principle

Divine Presence
'I AM'

Primal Matrix of Space
Containing the light seed
(in Man as the prototype
of all possibility).

Primal Energy
Source

Ray of Life as the line of
force from the monadic
presence.

Light seed or Christ Self Mobile
unit which acts as catalyst and
transformer, descending when
the frequencies of the lower
bodies invoke it and are
vibrationally fit to receive it.

(causal plane +
higher mental body)

Matter containing replica of
light seed as points of light
within the substance of the
three lower bodies.

Heart centre containing light
seed in manifestation in time
and space. Central post and
alchemical chamber.

LINEAR ALCHEMICAL ALIGNMENT 1B

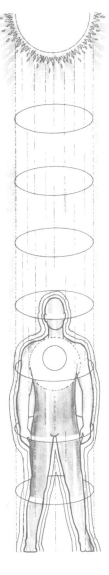

The main line of life force has widened with effort and continuous use, creating a real passageway or bridge, allowing greater and more intense energies to act.

Highest Vibrational Frequency

This phenomenon is only possible when the lower bodies are able to sustain higher frequencies at the level of matter, having worked consciously on the transmutation of matter (the absorption of karmic crystallizations) and on the expansion at the cellular level of the points of light which represent the multiple expression of the light seed in three dimensional substance.

This is the ALCHEMICAL TUBE OF LIGHT constucted with sustained invocation. When this passageway is activated the lower self is vibrationally raised to sustain the voltage of the higher self. Matter may be transmuted and the individual can attain to the consciousness of the causal plane.

The individual is One with the monad (Christed), able to channel, express and contain the energies and multiple facets of mankind.

Lowest Vibrational Frequency.

THE PROCESS OF EXPANSION OF LIFE:
THE REDEMPTION OF MATTER (KARMA)

As the points of light expand within matter, the vibrational level of the entire organism and its energetic field rises, amplifying heart centre irradiation and capacity. This is the picture of superior Man or of a master as an individuated Being.

Alchemical Chamber and electro-magnetic attraction point. Transformer and equalizer. Energy distributor through the points of light at the outpost of the elements throughout the body.

Points of light which are initially buried in dense matter coloured by polluted human thought-forms of incomplete experience.

The process of transmutation / expansion at the level of dense matter, or the activity of the points of light.

Structural transmutation at molecular levels:

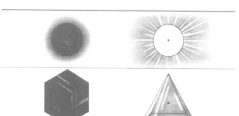

Structure of transmuted matter.

more weight

The lower self or the ordinary personality complex includes the three bodies of the personality: in other words the physical or biological structure, the mental complex and the emotional or nervous networks. The Christ Self uses the faculties of the higher mental body but represents the unit of the causal body. The Christ Self serves the function of gathering the energy descending (or emanating) from the source and adapting it for our use. In some esoteric literature this Christ Self is called the Solar Angel and is an individualized energy agent of tremendous proportions which acts as intermediary while the individual is creating his own causal nexus of transmuted matter and force.

The person on the path is gradually polarizing his structure of consciousness into depths and amplitudes which transcend the personality, stepping up the frequencies of his lower self complex. The Christ Self serves the function of inspiration and guidance, a perfected fount of vibrationally higher frequencies. The linear map depicts a way to linearly connect with the higher frequency of the Christ Self.

The 'I AM' Presence corresponds to the energy of the monad which is the light-seed within the Primal Matrix. It brings the subject closer to the realization that God is within, in the very 'I AM-ness' of being and not somewhere beyond its reach. It is the very heart of space within which we exist and have our being here and now in three-dimensional time and space.

Concentric force is an orgasmic activity occuring in man, stars, suns and galaxies. It is the very pulsation of life. It is birth and death. It is generation and absorption. It is chaos and implicit order. To be centred within it requires not only the cessation of compulsive thinking and emotional fluctuation, but also of doing itself. We cannot control it. We can only learn to flow and yield, poised and flexible within it.

Presenting both concentric and linear perspectives offers the very real advantage of being able to consciously access the activities that each depicts and which are present in every moment of our waking life. As a doer we utilize linear force through thought and activity, which represent the capacity to sustain concentric charge or life. As a being we live within concentric space and chaotic flow. By the time a person arrives at the state of individuation distinct from the animal-man that acts instinctively, he has the capacity not only to sustain but to redirect these forces; that is, for the elevation of the species and the enhancement of all of life.

At this point man is no longer bound by the law of karma, or cause and effect. He exists at the level of causality. He can now participate in the 'leela' of creation. He is in control and yet in the flow. He is in dominion.

Occultism reveals the laws of creation in time and space. The practices of Inner Alchemy provide the training ground for the vehicles as they prepare to sustain higher frequencies and begin to teach the individual how to act consciously and intelligently. Buddhist philosophy, with its eternal and immutable truths, reveals our essential state of being, free from trimmings and embellishments. The vision presented here offers a transitionary viewpoint which, when properly used, serves to connect us to the transcendental quanta of energy which are within us and in the universe. We learn to think in multiple and simultaneous ways.

Towards the One

The Absolute Is. It is both activity and repose. From Its Holy Spiritual womb as the Matrix springs the substance of creation. From Its Creator-force as the Father springs activity. Male and female are completely different expressions of the Absolute. In the human emotional experience of relationship the sexes represent individual manifestations of source-energy. Each needs to be lived fully in order to produce the unique flowering that each provides. Although we contain the other in seed form within, when the maturing process reaches its pinnacle of expression, the emerging androgynous creature is not bisexual. Its essence reaches beyond all duality and even beyond sex itself, while its vehicle remains to personify the perfection of Prototypical Man, the Christ Self, in each gender.

The real human is both potency and potential. This means that he is both the Absolute and the particular. Individual life evolves as matter evolves. This creates personal history, a history which will forever remain engraved in the very individuality file of the unit. The sum of experiences that we live, as the sub-personalities which we absorb and liberate, remain as facets on the diamond face of the jewel we become as Human, as Star, as Sun... Life cannot and does not efface itself into an amorphous mass; it acquires colouring and myriads forms. The very process of creating karma as we learn to manage and incorporate force and energy, creates individuality which later clothes the individuated being.

The very meaning of human life implies tension. This tension reflects the coexistence of both matter and light in a very real relationship that strives to expand into unlimited space. The human being, as a grain of sand in an ocean of virgin space, unites all polarities within himself and yet seeks to express a uniquely individualized version of the whole. When he integrates these polarities in neutrality, he performs the highest feat of alchemy: he neutralizes space into pure, eternal consciousness. As a human being on Earth he lived the discipline of material expression; as Superior Man upon the planet he begins to live the mastery of the soul.

We are too small to understand this yet. Let us pause, in silence, before the majesty and lessons of the heart.

Chapter Two

AS ABOVE, SO BELOW

Anyone who practises meditation has discovered that the inner world resembles the universe at large. This was known by the ancients at a time when outer and inner science were one and the same. From these observations arose Hermes Trismegistus' axiom which served as the basis for both medicine and astrology, and became the cornerstone of alchemy: As above, so below.

We seem to have lost the capacity to experience truth personally. This is due to the uncontrolled activity of the mind. Ordinary thinking creates waves which oscillate at faster, busier frequencies than those of any living thing. Geared to the denser properties of the world, this speed obstructs the perception of the greater nature vibrating in slower, more harmonious rhythms.

The individual on the path of self-knowledge and mastery becomes aware of energetic frequency variations as he learns control over his own mind, body and emotions. He may notice that as his material body relaxes, breathing slows down and awareness heightens. Relaxing both physically and mentally he becomes more sensitive to the universe around and within him. As awareness expands over the waking state it naturally carries over to the sleeping state as well. The organism becomes calm under the direct management of controlled multi-levelled awareness. The individual is present, in stillness, within concentric time and space. At this point the heart nexus, as a focus of consciousness, becomes the main organ of perception. Consciousness flows poised, within the chaotic pool of the primordial space matrix. Although our normal consciousness is not always aware of its multiple levels of experience, the activity of the space matrix perpetually unfolds multi-dimensional expressions.

In order for us to attain to levels of mastery over creation, we must simultaneously slow down our vegetative functions and prime up our awareness, in order to perceive, manage and interpret phenomena correctly. This means that we must master

our ability to focus consciousness at any one of the multiple levels and sustain awareness there. This requires an enormous amount of vital energy and an organism that
cooperates with the intention. It is not enough to relax, sleep or space out; one must
remain conscious, something which is very difficult for the ordinary person, who all
too easily loses awareness the moment he relaxes a little bit. I suggest students train
themselves to follow the thread of consciousness upon entering sleep and upon
awakening. This disciplines the mind to perceive and distinguish among subtle states
of reality. Observation such as this also teaches us to discriminate between thinking
activity and awareness. Our purpose is not to blot out awareness but to increase it.
It is not to dull but to heighten intelligent dominion and mastery over energy modulation. Good physical health is essential for this.

Breathing rhythms correspond to personality patterns. As an individual becomes
aware of his breathing imbalance he can take steps to change them. This corresponds to beginning work on destructuring the egoism of his personality. Egoism
cannot survive in states of harmony and equilibrium, energy and silence, which are
produced by balanced breathing.

Karma as personalistic energy crystallizations imbeds itself deeply into physical tissue, from where it catalyzes vortices of compulsive activity in emotional and mental
networks. The enhanced properties of light in the body caused by positive energy
modulation serve to purify the blood and clear the limbic (mental) system. The heart
centre, responding to light acceleration intensifies its irradiation. Then we can work
on the lower centres via the heart. The clearing and the cleaning up of karma is naturally intensified.

It is important we try to learn to sustain with awareness the intensities and varieties of stimulation that daily life provides, without falling prey to the limitations of
our psychology. As we train the concrete mind to perceive and to sustain harmony,
it pays off with an increased ability to translate and use concentric energies and realities. A broader vision of life opens up.

The Light Seed Pattern of the Microcosm

There is a greater state of being for each species or thing, superior to the manifested
form. This is the light seed or archetype which arises as an offspring from the Primal
Matrix. For us this light seed is the perfect pattern of the species known as Humanity.

The atom is the prime building block. Within its nucleus, perceivable as empty
space, we find a primordial speck of light. This contains the pattern of the unit.
Within each molecule, organism and system there lies a light seed. The nucleus is

constructed over and around it. The electrons which circulate on the periphery express its characteristics and are like the personality of the atom. Manifested form parts from the pattern set by the atom and expands infinitely. The simple and the multiple are the same in the universe as in man.

MOVEMENT OF THE ATOM OF CONSCIOUSNESS

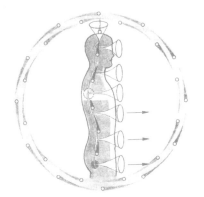

The atom of consciousness emerges when the 'atman' acquires a container for consciousness within the properties of the elements. As its life-sustaining quality descends into the base centre, creating a personality structure, its consciousness-inducing faculties are projected out into the world. They eventually return within upon the awakening of true spiritual reality.

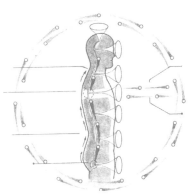

Polarization of the atom of consciousness at the causal level.

Point for the integration of consciousness.

Energy rises when the atom of consciousness is drawn inside, within the heart centre.

Projection of ideas into images. Emergence of the atom of consciousness.

Return of the atom of consciousness within. Reintegration of projected energies.

The energy from the elements at the level of the lower centres is projected outwards and then perceived through the faculties of the atom of consciousness. Now the individual interacting with the projections and through the positive use of the consciousness-inducing properties of the atom, can redeem the substance. Inversely, the individual can use the consciousness-inducing force of the atom negatively to energize and fixate thoughtforms, thus perpetuating illusion and creating more karma.

In the human body, the primordial light seed appears clairvoyantly like a minuscule sun. This point of light is the heart or life of the atom. In the same manner in which we expand consciousness, we also expand the activity of the points of light within each atom of physical substance. In this way we evolve the molecular structure to accommodate higher vibrational frequencies. The activity of this point of light determines the level of integrated applied consciousness.

The totality of points of light compose the body of light. This body of light is also called the etheric mould, the vital body and the mirror body, to name a few, but it must not be confused with the astral or the mental bodies. Both the astral and mental bodies have their own etheric mould reflected in this one.

The consciousness-activating process of the body of light penetrates within illusion, to produce a truly illumined and integrated vehicle. The individual may apply his disciplined will coupled with sensitivity into locating and expanding the activity of the points of light in his body, so that his anchored consciousness may be applied for the utilization of energies pertaining to multi-levelled realities.

The Dynamics of Awareness

The human energetic anatomy is a complex field of substance-energy. Awareness is the activity of intelligence as attention. Consciousness is a product of the two. The organism is a coordinated network of activity revolving around a primal seed of light. In the human being this seed is the 'atman'. It is considered to be the seat of consciousness located in the area of the third eye or pituitary gland. When the process of consciousness has been completed this point serves as the focus for the Unity of Consciousness. It is the repository of the blueprint, or Human Prototype. As its voltage is extremely high (attuned to cosmic intensities), it lies sealed and protected within the area of the brain until the entire organism arrives at the vibrational level where it can benefit from those frequencies which are multidimensional powers of perception and utilization of substance. Meanwhile, the process of evolution uses two other basic centres of activity: the heart centre and the base of the spine.

The heart centre feeds immediate life activities. The heart chamber is the seat for the permanent atoms of earth, water, fire and air, which coordinate the activity of the elements in the body.

Whereas at the heart centre life acquires a container within the substance of the elements, at the base of the spine the primary life-force, converted into denser etheric substance, is deposited for use by the human organism. It becomes the fount of life-sustaining vitality for the entire body and the basic reservoir for physical energy.

The real work of building illumined substance starts with the redemption of matter at the level of the basic chakra. Consciousness is fragmentary or illusory unless it is anchored in cellular experience. Once the experiences through the lower centres have been assimilated, the heart chamber prepares the individual for the quantum leap back to the fount of the Father represented by the energies pooled at the brow centre.

In this diagram, the seed (life) is embedded in matter, or the Mother. The symbol in the Orient for the basic centre (in both sexes symbolically) is a penis inside a vagina. In Eastern terminology this is seen as 'Heaven inside Earth'. The primordial Light Seed now contained within the basic, raw matter of the Earth. The human body in toto is the Earth. At its roots you have the male libido or seed, the sexual drive which triggers the activity of the mental and emotional counterparts of the element earth.

As consciousness increases, the molecules gradually change their basic composition from cubicular to pyramidal. The new shape of the molecules as they interact with one another in the heart chamber allows the intelligence within the element of air to begin constructing the causal body of consciousness and activates the faculties of the higher mental body.

The individual is better equipped now to continue the arduous journey of endless adaptation and application of spiritual principle. At the completion of this, consciousness becomes polarized at the throat centre - the repository of space itself - preparing to reach the light-emission centre at the third eye. When the individual eventually achieves integration here he becomes the 'Anthropos' or Perfect Human. In time, he blends with the multifaceted, multilevelled intelligence of the monad to express superior or Archetypal Man.

We can now see just how impersonal life force is injected into planetary substance and personalized through the experience of an individual human form. The consciousness within this individual body acquires personality as the energy from the heart centre projects through the lower centres, beginning at the base chakra. The phenomenon is later transformed into aspiration and applied will – the character and consciousness of the disciple. Character (the personality rendered conscious) and consciousness (represented by the amount of illumined or redeemed substance) will replace the primitive earthbound personality during the transition into a vaster consciousness, that of Man as the planetary Archetype of perfection. Such is the journey that every seeker faces: a journey against lower nature into Nature... a radical rupture of the molecular patterns of animal-man into the conscious creation of a man-god.

ANTHROPUS = TOTAL MAN

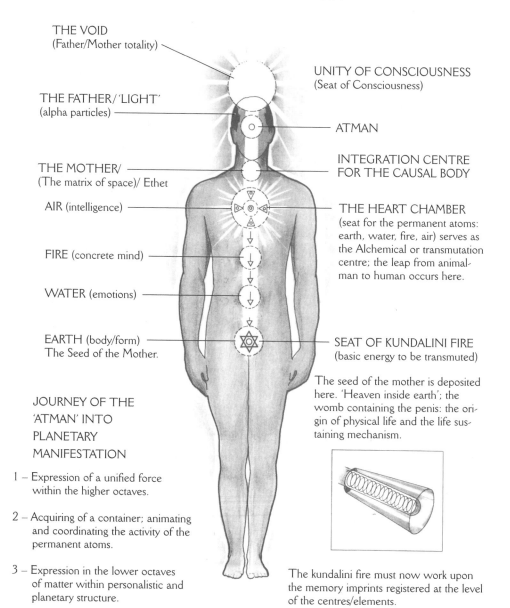

THE VOID
(Father/Mother totality)

UNITY OF CONSCIOUSNESS
(Seat of Consciousness)

THE FATHER/'LIGHT'
(alpha particles)

ATMAN

THE MOTHER/
(The matrix of space)/ Ethet

INTEGRATION CENTRE
FOR THE CAUSAL BODY

AIR (intelligence)

THE HEART CHAMBER
(seat for the permanent atoms:
earth, water, fire, air) serves as
the Alchemical or transmutation
centre; the leap from animal-
man to human occurs here.

FIRE (concrete mind)

WATER (emotions)

EARTH (body/form)
The Seed of the Mother.

SEAT OF KUNDALINI FIRE
(basic energy to be transmuted)

JOURNEY OF THE
'ATMAN' INTO
PLANETARY
MANIFESTATION

1 – Expression of a unified force
within the higher octaves.

2 – Acquiring of a container; animating
and coordinating the activity of the
permanent atoms.

3 – Expression in the lower octaves
of matter within personalistic and
planetary structure.

The seed of the mother is deposited
here. 'Heaven inside earth'; the
womb containing the penis: the origin of physical life and the life sustaining mechanism.

The kundalini fire must now work upon
the memory imprints registered at the level
of the centres/elements.

28

The Journey of the Atom of Consciousness

When the energy of the 'atman' originally descended into the heart centre it split into two modalites: one descending further to fertilize matter (the seat of consciousness), the other projecting outward to animate the intelligence-refining qualities of awareness (the atom of consciousness). During the life of an ordinary human being the atom of consciousness circulates around the periphery of the energy field surrounding the physical body. It is a luminous particle which is cast out into a world of common agreement. It appears at the same rate of vibratory activity corresponding to the thought processes of the individual. This means that if he is involved at the level of sexual preoccupation, his atom of consciousness appears low in his energy field, horizontal to the base centre. The energy triggered at the level of the lower centres will be outwardly absorbed and will colour the perception focused by the atom of consciousness, magnifying his interests. The same happens to the emotions when they hook into the soap-opera existence of most of humanity, or to the concrete mind when it attunes itself with the concern for power of the ambitious masses. This is the mechanism of thinking as it moves within collective subconsciousness and the consciousness of detail in the world.

As the process of self-awareness deepens the person begins to dissolve or disenergize these projected thoughtforms which usually involve entanglements with people in relationships and situations. Redirecting the energy requires resolving outer issues with a maximum of integrity. This means embracing the lessons which his projections and involvements provided. This usually includes tremendous suffering and demands consummate courage. Imprisoned energy from the thoughtforms releases power which liberates the essential self. Simultaneous to this awakening to his real self, molecular transmutation occurs.

The energy released by the thoughtforms returns to the heart chamber in degrees. Here it is recorded within the memory files of the permanent atoms as consciousness. The heart centre now exerts a magnetic attraction for the energy of the lower centres, which rises up through the spine to merge with the energies of their corresponding permanent atom at the heart. The atom of consciousness itself does not move up the spine. What moves up the spine is the energy that had been residing in the basic centres now freed from the hold of unprocessed desire.

The rising energetic potential is not a process which can be forced by the will; it is something that happens as a result of integrated consciousness (meaning body, mind and emotions). This must be simultaneously confirmed in the individual's outer

Chapter Three

MATTER & CONSCIOUSNESS

The Building Activity of Light

Life springs out of the unmanifest primordial darkness as light. Everything in manifestation is a result of this light, which is also known as universal mind. Light, in its multiple spherical expressions of colour and sound-waves modifies by degrees into the worlds of existence until it appears as filaments. As these filaments weave themselves into textures, they give birth to substances of light and then to matter.

Light travels through space as an emission, engendering what is called will or intent. Such was the journey of the 'atman' into the seat of consciousness. This will aspect of the manifested light evokes and sustains life and as substance becomes the line of force upon which matter is spun. In the human body this line of force condenses into the spinal column, and through the reproductive impulse of life there arise the skeletal, nervous and circulatory systems which conduct and adapt life force throughout the human organism.

Secondly, light illumines the form with a self-sustaining activity, a potential for intelligence and a capacity in the human to know itself. Such was the phenomenon of the atom of consciousness. Light energizes matter so that it may acquire experience and form an identity which will create yet more forms. The third activity of light is to fertilize matter in such a way as to give birth to different functions and configurations of intelligence within form. In this way light expresses itself as the elements and nourishes the various forms of elemental life in the physical world which we know as nature.

Everything in creation, in the microcosm as in the macrocosm, reveals the activity of light in this triune form, corresponding to the continual activity of the three primary rays. These three rays constitute the building process within all forms.

In ordinary human life, the three rays inspire the three bodies of the personality:

the physical body, the emotional network and the mental structure. As long as our awareness is held at the level of projection, our body will be conditioned by the laws of elemental life, our emotions will react to the stimuli is around us, and our minds will reveal the collective mentality of the time and culture we belong to. If, however, the individual directs himself inwardly, he begins to partake of a different kind of law, the law of grace, or light. At those levels, which I have called dimensions in my first book, man's perception witnesses light formations, is overwhelmed by intense and unknown qualities of love, ecstasy and power, and is inspired by concepts, ideas, symbols and archetypes which convey a more abstract and unifying function of mind.

When we try to locate the perceptual apparatus which cognites and corresponds to higher, subtler sensibilities within the physical organism, we find that it relates to the intuiting activity of the upper centres. These centres stock and develop the faculties of the three rays and constitute the upper triad. The three lower centres governing matter and gravity are called the lower triad. The material in this book deals mainly with the mechanisms of the lower triad, which is the world of relationship.

Energy and Force

Light as vital solar energy feeds all living things. It enters into planetary space through the sun's emission, conveying and releasing numerous particles of cosmic origin.

The particles which access and sustain life arrange themselves into two basic sub-atomic patterns. The human organism is composed of atomic structures, which are the result of the attraction-repulsion interplay between certain sub-atomic particles. This gives birth to what in esoterism is called force – vital force. Intelligence, on the other hand, that which produces consciousness, relates to sub-atomic electronic particles which do not operate by polarity but rather through a symmetrical law of syntony, which is called by esoteric science electronic energy.

The atoms and particles which underly organic matter are of an asymmetrical order; they co-exist separately, together with another particle of opposite charge: electrons (–) with protons (+). As these particles combine they form strong atomic units of larger and larger proportions, forming molecules which also group under the same law of attraction and repulsion, or separate coexistence within the compound they create. If this extremely tense relationship is upset in any way, the stability of the compound is broken or disturbed to such extent as to cause the dissolution of the substance. This annhiliation releases tremendous power through atomic fission. The principle behind nuclear bombs is the same as behind cellular transmutation. Our normal relationships also work on this principle.

The kind of sub-atomic particles which operate under the symmetrical patterns in esoterism are related to human intelligence and consciousness. They combine in intimate cohesion through syntony of movement. These particles, which are the result of the encounter of electrons (−) with other electrons of positive charge (called positrons) manifest themselves as light or photons. Electrons are always emitting and absorbing when they meet other electrons. Photons and virtual photons have neither positive nor negative charge. According to esoterism, photons are responsible for much of the healing and imaging properties. Science and modern technology uses the symmetric properties of light in laser technology and holography, and in the emergence of superfluids and superconductors. The light we see springs when the positrons and electrons meet. This meeting, which marks the birth of light is entirely different from the process which occurs to form organic and inorganic matter. The identity of the positron and electron is entirely absorbed and they are transmuted into photons or two particles of light. The principle behind the emergence of light is the law governing the cosmos. Analogically, in relationships a higher order of things can only come about when the lower individual identity (or egoism) ceases altogether.

We could say that the points of light at the centre of each atom mentioned in the preceding chapter belong to the symmetrical group of cosmic dancers, as does the atom of consciousness (which is not an atom in the material sense). These particles of light give off electronic energy and conduct life-source into matter. The asymmetrical dancers release a different kind of energy, called bio-energy or force, in the case of living beings. Within the human organism we find both force and energy in their pure forms and as an interactive process. Transmutation occurs when energy acts upon force, overtaking the rhythm imposed by matter. This mechanism transmutes the conflicting and separatistic individualities within the atomic relationship, releasing an irradiatory quality that we here call consciousness.

The harmonious (separate-but-equal) competition prevailing at sub-atomic levels of matter is what Pauli has termed the 'Principle of Exclusion' and dictates the behaviour not only of matter but of the subtle aspects of matter which we call psychology. Human relationships mirror that mechanism, acting out and perceiving in mutual exclusion until the phenomenon of light upsets the dichotomy of collective elemental behaviour. Collective elemental behaviour is predicated on polarity and judgment, such as attachment and aversion, either/or, and good/bad, and not on true wholistic perception. This is the reason why we can say that most of humanity is still at the level of animal-man.

Regardless of all the sweet-talk about love and altruism, we continue to love someone or something and at the same time (in the name of that love) hate someone or something else, both feelings existing simultaneously. The love which is coincidentally real understanding (wisdom) exists only without polarity, outside the range of emotional contradictions and mental justifications. The body organism and its counterpart, the unconscious personality, are dictated by the rhythms of subconscious life. True light has no power to direct it. When matter is redeemed, on the other hand, it begins to respond to the law prevailing over electronic energy. The collective force dictating a collective subconscious mechanism ceases to be the compelling dynamic and individuated (or integrated) activity arises. Compulsive behaviour becomes creativity and conscious loving. Individual activity is now directed by light or universal mind. Vital force and spiritual energy are mutually exclusive... until they fuse within man in the transmutation process of the alchemy of consciousness.[4] The real spiritual journey begins when we start to focus upon light as the governing principle. Our concrete mind ultimately controls the movement of the atom of consciousness and also has the power to redirect the automatic activity of the lower forces. Its frequency (located at the solar plexus) is superior to the lower two. It is here where the light particles begin to evoke and merge with the light from the heart centre.

Where there is life there is energy, but only in man does electronic energy appear in a pure form, offering a kind of subliminal pull or memory-without-content which constitues the potential for Self-awareness, and the driving force towards fulfilment. In the animal and lower forms of life, energy is immediately and automatically converted into vital force. There is no structure in plants or animals for light to operate independently or to be stocked in abeyance within the upper centres as it is in the individual human.

In order for electronic energy to feed and sustain life at the lower centres as it does in animals, another passageway, unique in man, acts as conduit. This is the silver cord, consisting of a series of light filaments strewn together to form a cord. This cord sustains life and revitalizes the organism directly into the outpost at the solar plexus. The body automatically converts this energy into force to sustain life activities, including its mental and emotional machinery. If the person is still under the grip of the lower instincts, this energy which was destined to fuel consciousness only serves to aggravate unconscious personality characteristics such as anger, fear, desire, hatred and the many emotional thoughts a human-animal is capable of. Unless the person's heart predominates and the person has strengthened his will constructively, the automatic programming of his own biology will only accentuate the lower passions. Unless a person's conscious qualification is involved, all the tricks of the New Age, including invocations, affirmations, and the many evocation practices of light will most surely catalyze the forces of the lower centres, creating more and more fantasy, illusion, devotional hysteria and sentimentality, pompousness and pride, serving to augment the already polluted astral dimension and clouding the possibility for true individual perception.

Life in Expression

Let us understand that light has no awareness; it simply is. The basis of initiatic science is the creation of illumined matter (consciousness) through the transmutation of atomic molecules into light. In returning to the source, that light becomes amplified through awareness of itself, bridging the worlds of unconsciousness with the possibility of light. In achieving the state of 'anthropus' or perfect master, Man becomes a creator with the full knowledge of his essence and his power.

The three or primary rays, as one, create life. The remaining four rays emanate from the three-as-one and represent qualifications of life, modalities in which life expresses itself. Each of the seven rays emanates from the central light and together form the backbone of all creation. They provide, the energetic impulse around which life is spun. Through the spinal column, (our main line of force), the ascending spiral of the evolutionary process rises from the lower centres and also through it the descending impulse of electronic energy spirals downwards as inspiration and energy. Energy and force meet at the midway station in the heart. The centres above the heart act as warehouses for the stocking of electronic energies; the centres below act as natural outposts for the expression of the elements.

Light enters the human organism through the head and cuts through the entire body, adapting itself first at the level of the third eye, at the throat centre, and then at the heart centre (where it acquires a container that enables it to launch itself out into the world as the atom of consciousness), and finally descends into the base centre. Light also activates the centres which are responsible for the building of consciousness, providing us with substance and faculties at the level of the chakras.

The chakras are centres for the absorption and processing of elemental substance in modalities which provide lessons. The light filaments through the chakras act upon elemental matter of different mineral, vegetable and animal origins, recreating the process of evolution itself, a process which we use for whatever purposes we consciously or unconsciously evoke. Coloured by the rays, each element relates to a level of planetary life, and is symbolically related to each of the elements of nature which serves as a working laboratory for consciousness. As the elements lend themselves to man, man in turn has the responsability and obligation to enhance or elevate the consciousness in them through the process of his own refinement. We use the power and faculty we acquire through the experience of each element to build our character in the world.

ELECTRONIC ENERGY

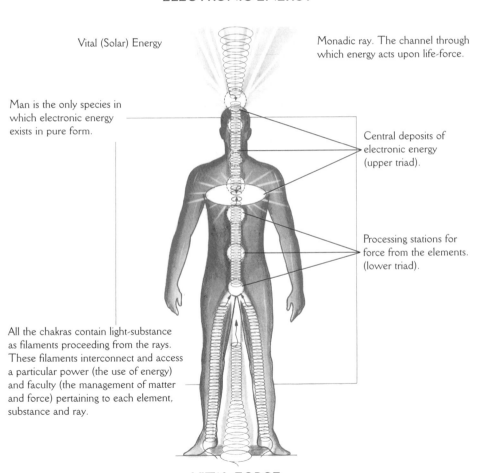

Vital (Solar) Energy

Monadic ray. The channel through which energy acts upon life-force.

Man is the only species in which electronic energy exists in pure form.

Central deposits of electronic energy (upper triad).

Processing stations for force from the elements. (lower triad).

All the chakras contain light-substance as filaments proceeding from the rays. These filaments interconnect and access a particular power (the use of energy) and faculty (the management of matter and force) pertaining to each element, substance and ray.

VITAL FORCE

The Elements and the Spirits of Nature

Following the atomic model, the planet Earth is a unit of the Solar System and the Solar System itself is a unit of the Milky Way. Inversely, we ourselves are atomic units within the body of the Earth. The elements within our body resonate with the elements of the planet as with the causes in the universe.

Each element has a spirit and personality of its own, but each also responds to the directing will of man. Elements exist as a constant building activity, an endless cyclical movement which we perceive within ourselves as life-death-rebirth, and outwardly as the changes of the seasons. The purpose of this activity is to continually bring harmony and balance in the world. We often fail to see just how this works.

The eternal and universal law of energy dictates that the higher travels towards and commands the lower. Endowed with the capacity to contain and manipulate energy through our atom of consciousness, we are in the unique position to manage and direct the nature spirits of the elements, who instantly respond to our mental processes. As our will is used mostly subconsciously, the elements tend to manifest thier imbalances within our bodies and over the general environment. We need to understand that the power we have over the elements is the opportunity we have to use the vital force and substance which they provide in the building of our body of consciousness. As we build consciousness, we refine the body of the planet.

Without the elements we have no power, no faculties, no matter with which to build the body of consciousness, no territory within which to act, nothing with which to practise our abilities and learn to command, handle and manipulate substance, energy and force. What makes us human is the life that lives through us, the potential which seeks to express itself, and the opportunity that we have to create ourselves. In order to take a leap from animal-man to Perfect Human, we evolve through matter into a spiritual activity that we create. In order to truly become Human we must apply the alchemical law which states: you can only transform lead into gold if you have some gold. This gold is the activity of light within the heart, expressing itself as the potential for true reasoning ability.

Our gold mine is our stock of electronic energy which, as we saw, can only be used when it has a centre from which to operate and a field of substance to act upon. That centre is the acknowledgement that 'I AM (in my 'I ness') THE LIGHT, THE POWER AND THE GLORY...' That field of substance is the matter of the very earth we tread, and which pulsates within our vehicles as life. We have come, by and large, to bow before the majesty of the POWER and the GLORY, but we have overlooked a simple and obvious body of peons without which there would be no way to express the POWER and the GLORY: the body of the elements which compose, build and run our organism and colour our psychology.

We could say that the process of becoming human entails cooperation with each of the elements and the conscious use of the powers or faculties which each of them provide. The process of purification represents the succesful assimilation of those powers and faculties in such a way as to contain and manipulate the substance of the elements in a new expression.

Personality building entails cooperation; purification implies disidentification with the power acquired. In order to find our Self, we must have lost ourself. The arena of relationships offers just this opportunity. Every relationship in the outer world reflects a relationship in the inner world with the elemental consciousness involved, and every elemental consciousness teaches us the management of a certain aspect of vital force.

CREATION OF THE ATOM OF CONSCIOUSNESS
AROUND A LINE OF FORCE

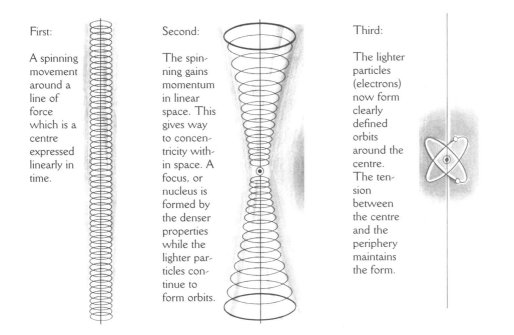

First:

A spinning movement around a line of force which is a centre expressed linearly in time.

Second:

The spinning gains momentum in linear space. This gives way to concentricity within space. A focus, or nucleus is formed by the denser properties while the lighter particles continue to form orbits.

Third:

The lighter particles (electrons) now form clearly defined orbits around the centre. The tension between the centre and the periphery maintains the form.

Earth

The gnomes are the elementals which handle what are called the 'chemical ethers', or all that pertains to the element of earth. Physically, this element is represented by the whole body. The base chakra organizes tissue and determines the form aspect, including the spine and skin. The element of earth also extends to our creation of all forms in the outside world.

The spleen and pancreas, the stomach and the muscular structure itself relate to the element of earth. Each of these, as well as the whole body composite, respond to our way of relating to the concept within earth. This implies the management of everything that is of the earth, including money and possessions. Excess of any sort will lead to a malfunction in our body or in our world. This world includes our own emotional and mental life.

The gnomes are said to be extremely practical and resourceful. They symbolize the utmost in measure and conservation, while at the same time representing abundance. More than any other elemental they have suffered under humanity's selfishness and ruthlessness, embodying at times the very opposite of their qualifications. Humanized, they can be extremely miserly, hoarding, greedy and sour. They are the elementals which most resemble man in appearance and psychology, mimicking our gestures and physiognomy. Their energies ricochet upon persons who violate the most subtle genetic substance through sexual abuse or promiscuity.

In order to master the element of earth and all that pertains to it, we need to honour all the positive attributes that are contained within it. In this way we embrace the qualities of the gnomes, passing on to inherit all the characteristics and faculties which the element earth possesses.

Water

Undines are the elementals directing the 'ether of life', as the element of water. In our physical bodies this element rules the kidneys, bladder and in some systems the bones. It's centre of activity is the second chakra, reflecting our emotional management and predisposition.

Our emotions become outpictured in our body, in our relationships and in our physical surroundings. Water serves as the womb of creation and all forms arise from within it. It rules over our reproductive organs and our sexual activity, reflecting in our capacity for receptivity and sympathy. Undines have been known to offer real life water dangers to people who indulge in self-pity and depression. Imitating us, undines can emit selfish and sexually deviate energies. They have also come to influence and stand for false psychism, the kind that occurs when feelings are projected onto reality. In order for us to pass through the tests of this element and gain mastery over it we must stand for integrity and truthfulness, sensitivity and consideration with our fellow men and our surroundings. We must be able to feel deeply and yet not become lost in our feeling. This is perhaps the most important lesson in the art of relationship and dominion over the self.

Fire

Fire is called the 'reflective ether' because it reflects the worlds of light with its multi-dimensional magnificence and power and is closely connected to the solar source itself. The fire elementals are called salamanders and are the only elementals that are trans-dimensional. This means that they live considerably longer and exert an influence upon several dimensions of reality simultaneously, from the physical fire to the violet flame, from the tiny salamander to the splendid archangelic figures of the fiery worlds. It is they who bridge the activities of the solar plexus and the heart by igniting the fire of intuition.

The physical organ which connects with these powers is, of course, the heart, although functionally the solar plexus as a generator is also involved. The endocrine glands, the blood and the blood vessels are ruled by the element of fire, as is the small intestine, and indirectly the liver, gallbladder and nerves (which in the Chinese system belong to what they call the element 'wood').

Salamanders are immensely creative, possessing strong attributes of ardour, valour, energy and fidelity, all of which are needed by us if we wish to conquer ourself. In the negative modalities salamanders are destructive, bossy, unfaithful and cowardly. They consume coleric persons who throw tantrums, and can go so far as to cause burns and fire accidents to these people.

Air

Reigning over the element of air, the sylphs represent intelligence, and communication, ability to witness with detachment and speed. The sylphs manage the 'ether of light', which means anything that pertains to the workings of the mind and the light of consciousness. In its opposite expression the sylphs, in their effort to accommodate man's habits, can express cruelty and instability, shrewdness and intellectualism. They can manage to cause falls and broken bones to undiscerning or mentally sluggish people.

The physical body processes and reflects the activity of the element air through the lungs and large intestines, and in some systems the skin as well, which furnishes the cellular structure with an automatic breathing function. At moments when the aspirant is struggling to acquire dominion over the incessant chatter of the mind, he may find himself unable to face the wind – somehow feeling weakened by it. When we acquire a certain level of mastery over our own thoughts, we find a mysterious resonance with all the expressions of the element air, which appear, to grant us all its powers and abilities.

This element represents the beginning and also the end stages of the seeker as he strives to refine his mind, and then to integrate his experiences. This happens within what is called the lower chamber of the heart, the area between the solar plexus and the heart chakra itself.

Every time the individual sets upon working on himself the elementals shift restlessly until he can regroup and harmonize them. During each step, as in each initiation, readjustment is called for. As we grow in consciousness and are able to handle a certain amount of intensity, more energy will be made available, calling for greater and greater lessons in flexibility. The path of initiation includes the mastery over all the elements.

Our relationship with the elements is recorded in the permanent atom for each of the elements within the heart chamber. They contain personal history in the form of vibrational capacity. Each time we master a certain element, the capacity we acquire to sustain the frequencies releases the powers and faculties within that element for our use. This is like saying that when a person is able to control the force of the lower centres, harnessing rather than dispersing, his consciousness is able to access the permanent atoms themselves. Then we have enough faculty, power and momentum to literally reconstruct our body and our life.

KALEIDOSCOPE

Mind, Meaning and Projection

Mind takes on a linear modality when it is casting light upon the elements and gathering experience, at the level of the lower centres. Inversely it takes on the concentric modality when it acts through the upper centres in a pure form. The first is called the lower or concrete mind; the second is what is known as the higher mind. The placement of the atom of consciousness determines perception – our living reality or dimension.

During the personality phase of development, the activity of mind is horizontally active, reflecting the collective mind of humanity. There is no way through which to communicate with someone whose experience is based solely on collective horizontal modalities, that is consensus reality, the perception of multidimensional frequencies. Only the quality of lived time and the variety of it can bring about understanding.

Life is everywhere. The manner in which it presents itself is always and continually a kaleidoscopic play of perspectives. As we turn the kaleidoscope we can always wonder at what we see and what we become, as we readjust to the dance of light and colour, form and sensation which we continually reinterpret as mind plays the game of life.

In Mastery, the Path of Inner Alchemy, I proposed a map of consciousness which covered twelve levels of vibratory activity which are seen as dimensions or qualities of inner reality. We could say that our experience does not usually reach beyond the third dimension. If our mental instrument has been sharpened by training in scientific rationale, such as logic or mathematics, we may at times delve into the fourth, fifth and sixth dimensions of expression to access universal mind as it manifests on those levels, and translate that into third dimension terminology and application. A few remarkable people go beyond. Jung was able to reach into the seventh dimension. Mystics and enlightened individuals may rise even beyond that.

Because there are not many geniuses like Einstein and Jung, the mass of humanity only fantasizes that it perceives subtle realities which are actually projections of its desires onto astral phenomena within the third dimension itself. It is in this way that we obtain our so-called channelled 'communiqués' and how astral energies are shaped to influence eluded seekers who don't know how to deal with their personal reality.

The ambition which is at the root of unprocessed vitality also fosters ideas about survival which are inappropriate. In order to dissipate the illusion that the petty human egoism might be glorified and ascend to the heights, please understand that unless the entire unit of the three bodies (physical, mental and emotional) has been integrated, real consciousness or perception is not possible.

As sustained heart-centred consciousness, light functions at a frequency which is higher than most humans are able to withstand. For this reason the average human is never able to utilize energy in the ultimate creative task of anchoring conscious-ness. And yet, once we have experienced light, even in its humblest and mildest expressions, there is no turning back. Light ultimately creates its own meaning and becomes more important than the little self.

As mentioned previously, we exist in multiple dimensions simultaneously, but we do not live consciously within them until we have sorted out our third-dimensional reality and trained ourselves to perceive and move deliberately within them. In our relationships, particularly the truly loving ones, we often access our liasons at higher levels and connect with currents of blissful serenity which are the hallmark of love.

THE SEVEN BODIES OR ENERGY FIELDS

Original terminology used in Inner Alchemy		Usual occult terminology
Electronic	The Self	Monadic
Causal		Atmic
Higher Mental		Buddhic
Etheric	the Human Prototype or Light Seed	Causal
Mental		Mental
Astral	The lower bodies of planetary substance and collective activity	Astral
Physical (and vital mould)		Physical (Etheric or vital mould)

Inversely, we also contact memory imprints from negative experiences which underlie antipathy and irritation. These mechanisms are outlined in this book. The explanation of the dimensions themselves are contained in my first book.

When our vibratory field of activity shifts into a more accelerated rate, our perception uncovers another world or dimension. But the same applies inversely. We are our own heaven and our own hell. Only a perfect master, one who has constructed his own causal nexus, is immortal. At the moment, we are living through thought formations and accumulating impulses which must seek resolution by like vehicles or frequencies. In this way all the karmic issues which we must resolve, and which are accumulated in the memory banks of our genes and atmosphere, must be resolved through experience.

Perception

As each monadic seed and sub-seed acquires a vehicle of expression in the lower forms, so too does it form finer vehicles of perception, but these lie in waiting until the causal modality is ignited within the heart. There are seven bodies or energetic fields surrounding the human form. Each form has an irradiatory activity related to higher dimensional activity. One can distinguish the lower (astral) thoughtforms from the higher (spiritual) by their vibrational frequency.

The main bodies of activity for the ordinary human being are the three bodies of the personality. Inside these three bodies, which lie within and mildly emanate around the physical, lies the etheric mould which contains the memory bank from the genes and environmental conditions, the pattern of the mental and emotional bodies, and also the seed of light. This compound etheric body is highly sensitive and contains the basic circuitry of the filaments of light woven together to form the chakras and other lines of force interconnecting the body parts and functions. The aura of a human being is composed largely by the etheric emanations of the three lower bodies of elemental vital force.

The causal body or buddhic web resembles an egg and emanates from around the heart compound. It is the outer edge of the seed which contains the Human Archetype. Conscious or unconscious, this buddhic field is property, as light substance, of the monadic cell and is extremely vulnerable to the misqualifications which we provoke at the level of the lower self. This means that each transgression of the law of nature, such as neglect, indulgence in excesses of the personality, (elementals) which are the very substance of karma. Each individual creates his own variants upon the matter of his vehicles superimposed over the elemental structures inherited from his geneology. Remember, the matter of the vehicles is not ours; our own history predetermines the quality of materials. Some materials are purer or clearer than others.

If, for example, in my family background there has been a free-flowing non-inhibiting and dignified code of behaviour suggested regarding sexuality (as there is in some remote Polynesian and South American Indian cultures), both the physical matter and the psychological expression of sexuality will be spontaneous and pure. If there is a cultural history of puritanism and condemnation, the psychological modali-

CONSCIOUSNESS EXPRESSION

The position of the chakras and the radiatory activity at the level of consciousness reached when the anterior and posterior activity is balanced and 'centred'.

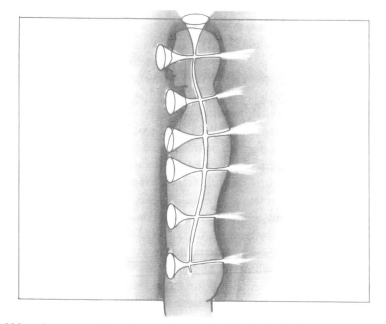

When the process of consciousness is completed at the level of each chakra, the resulting emanation of consciousness is uniform in both directions: world activity and inner discernment.

ties of the individual will already contain a good dosage of prejudice and a fanatical predisposition which will most likely accentuate repression and condemnation, creating what is known as compulsions or obsessions. As a general rule, all three lower centres of humanity are covered by adherences created by the collective unconscious, with relative clearings in some individuals.

The largest and densest clusters of adherences in the body of humanity are in the area of the genitals, legs and feet (which are extensions of the base chakra, with the exception that they also represent the ability to stand on one's own two feet). This is the most damaged area of humanity's body for obvious reasons.

The next largest and densest area is around the head, literally clouding real vision and insight. The upper centres, besides being vibrationally inaccessible to most people, are at the receiving end of euphemized projections from the lower centres. For example, everything that through desire an individual believes (third chakra activity) is spiritual (disguised sexual impulse, or first chakra) is projected onto more socially acceptable expressions which are located above (in the upper centres). In this way we have what are basically anger and violence appearing as religious fanaticism, and frustrated sexual fulfilment appearing as sublimated communion with so-called beings of light.

In this upper region we often see pretty bubbles of light side-by-side with monstrous dark clouds in front of the third-eye region, the throat and the crown. The pretty bubbles are benign collective thoughtforms called belief and dogma which although basically harmless to others, still limit flexibility and obstruct perception of the real. At the heart level there may be a little spark of true light if the individual has a genuine aspiration towards inner communion. In most cases the heart is blocked by emotional ambitions, fears and repressions.

The chakras are hardly ever functioning in their true and individual potential but in combination with other chakras. There are correllations between lower and higher expressions. Both the second and throat chakras pertain to creativity. Both the solar plexus and third eye relate to vision and intelligence. Both the heart and crown centres connect to electronic energies. A person's projected 'spirituality' augments the proportion of adherences upon the upper correlate of the chakra.

Each of the chakras presents a lesson that can only be learned in relationship with the world, as it pertains to the right development of personality in alignment with higher values. The stage is set when the energy which seeks to be integrated reaches out and finds the corresponding energies outside which will help it to express itself and force a resolution. Here follows a description of the qualities and possibilities within each chakra at the level of the individual.

Not all of the manifestations which reflect the processing activity at the level of the

When this centre's activity is thwarted, causing it to become absorbant rather than radiatory, the ensuing symptoms express superficiality, phoneyness and suicidal tendencies. The positive attributes at this stage include tolerance and trust in inner light. Here the taste in foods will be simple, with a major emphasis on aesthetics. This contrasts sharply with the taste in foods at the level of the solar plexus, which were sweets and carbohydrates and everything that would give quick energy to the organism. Here sleep patterns vary from nine to sixteen hours of sleep at night, depending on the time needed for inner attunement, assimilation, and regeneration.

Perception here is overwhelmed with a sense of timelessness as the causal modality seeks to link up to electronic frequencies. The classic manifestation, when intuition erupts prematurely within an intellectually undeveloped (concrete) mind, is a mental blackout. This happens as the linearity of the concrete mind gives way into the concentric perceptions which occur at a level beyond duality. At this moment one does not seem to be able to find verbal expressions to convey the experience of the heart. Another higher function of the mind comes into being.

Higher Mind serves itself of the structures learned and mastered by the lower mind but is ruled by the flexibility of the intuition of the heart. This is the true, or real Mind, which will lead to the development of the third eye. There, true intelligence is marked by simplicity, spontaneity, synthesis and holistic visionariness. A person who has not processed the forces at the level of the heart will always manifest judgmentalism, rigidity, complexity and seriousness: trademarks of egoism.

There arises here a need for physical expression which is very different from that of the basic chakra. Rather than a yearning of skin upon skin, the attraction here is wider and more refined, such as that sensed through the fingertips and through the entire energy field in an embrace that overflows into emotional and mental expressions as well. At this level emotions become empathy and deep understanding. The individual inspires creativity, feeling a nurturing and nourishment within his own wholeness and the growing communion with modalities of light, while also radiating that quality to others. Awareness moves beyond the self-involvement of the second chakra and the ambitiousness of the third to find itself in a relationship with the emerging reality of the higher self.

This is probably why all esoteric traditions emphasize the qualities of this centre, the place where the unconscious personality dissolves and the causal nexus is constructed as a replacement for self-conscious expression. In this manner there appear to be two distinct functions or 'chambers' of the heart: the one where the fire of the lower instincts merges in the process of consumption; the other where the light produced by the transmutation of fire expresses itself in emerging causal modalities.

The Fifth Chakra: Transcendence

This chakra is centred at the throat, influencing sound expression, and communication, hearing, telepathy and all esoteric uses of sound and the word. It also serves as the seat for the causal body built at the level of the heart. The causal modality becomes polarized here. When the integrated forces from the lower centres serve the higher will, the power available at this level of consciousness is tremendous. This is the centre utilized in invocation, mantras, decrees and alchemical formulas. But these formulas will not work in the manner in which they are meant to unless the connection to substance at the level of the lower forces has been made subservient to the intelligence of consciousness.

There is another reason why this centre is also the base for operations of the higher self; it is the meeting place for the three upper chakras (which comprise another centre as well). This elevated function has been called the 'Bindu' or 'Jade Gate', which means 'Bliss Pool' or the 'Mouth of God'. The powers collect at the base of the brain, looping from the centre of the throat, through the third eye, the crown and back down to the base of the skull.

When the atom of consciousness passing through the inner channels of the spine activates this centre, the voice takes on a melodious tone, harmonious and beautiful, conveying the range of human emotions and aspirations and evoking higher truth. Energy at this level becomes nurture through sound, much like a mother's gentle lullaby. The symbol for this centre in the East is the Mother and Child, representing that reception from above which enables us not only to survive at the higher vibratory levels, but to recreate ourself. Western occultists have also called this centre the cornucopia centre, meaning that whatever is expressed through the voice can become a manifest reality.

The prime connection here is with primordial, as yet unmanifest substance. This is what is known as the 'matrix of space', expressing itself as sound, the 'voice of intuition' or 'clairaudience'. True clairaudience is the etheric reverberation of love generated in the heart which accesses the primordial stuff of creation.

On the opposite spectrum, a permanently shrill and disharmonic voice can reveal lack of consciousness and often points to the misuse of the prime gift of this centre which is to use the voice (or sound) to bless. As one learns to nourish oneself with the substance of light, one affects in like manner through sound vibrations, one's environment.

The fifth chakra rules the thyroid, the bronchial and vocal apparatus, the lungs and the alimentary canal. In oral sex, the higher frequencies of the centre are often

THE SEVEN CHAKRAS –
FUNCTIONS OF CONSCIOUSNESS AT THE PHYSICAL LEVEL

Chakra	Attributes	Rays
First	Use of personal will. Purity. Commitment to the planet. Responsibilty. Security. Grounding (base of spine and legs).	Fourth
Second	Invocation. Sensitivity to vibration (supersensitivity). Individuality. Balance between the social and the personal.	Seventh
Third	Mobility. Personal control. Peace. Fearlessness. Generosity. Balance. Ability to set limits. Time. Travel. Orderliness and co-operation.	Sixth
Fourth	Divine Love. Tolerance. Forbearance. Trust Being 'in touch with self'. Unconditional love. Timelessness. Joining consciousness and matter.	Third
Fifth	Divine will. Power to create. Expression and communication. Hearing, telepathy, time and space travel. Cornucopia.	First
Sixth	The all-seeing eye. Concentration and consecration. Clairvoyance. Order and will. The future.	Fifth
Seventh	Invocation. Knowing. The Christ Self. No limits. Cosmic consciousness. Oneness. Power of transmutation.	Second

Note: The upper three chakras, i.e. the 5th, 6th and 7th join at the base of the brain and function as a unit at the level of interdemensional activity. In ancient times, this part of the brain was called the Bindu, Jade Gate or Bliss Pool.

Negative Reactions/Needs*

Alienation and jumpiness. Needs 12 hrs sleep, heavy foods, violence.

Hysteria. Sensuality (pleasure/pain). Acting now for future, loud music, spices, 10 hrs sleep.

Untogetherness, inability to say 'no'. Tendency to power-trip: control through domination or submission. Jealousy. Needs sugars and 8 hrs sleep

Sense of emptiness. Suicidal. Acting 'nice'. Judgmental Craves simple foods and 9 to 16 hrs sleep.

Confusion. Alienating others. Putting the self down. Can trasmute all foods and partake of any sleep pattern.

Illogical, over-intellectual. Spaced-out. Introversion, forgetfulness, fearful of future.

No faith. A sense of being controlled or possessed.

Bodies Affected/Senses

Kidneys, adrenals, spinal column. Physical. Sense of smell and sensations.

Etheric. Sense of taste. Gonads, reproductive system.

Emotional. The nervous system. Sight. Gall bladder. Pancreas. Stomach

Electronic and higher mental. Thymus and circulatory system. Heart, Blood, Vagus nerve. Touching.

Casual. Sense of hearing, the thyroid and the vocals. Bronchials, lungs and alimentary canal.

Lower and higher mental bodies. Left brain, left eye, ears nose and nervous system. Pituitary.

Casual and electronic and dimensions beyond. The upper brain and the right eye. Pineal.

*When the pure attributes are not integrated.

is indigo, a colour which heals, activates and further stimulates the higher faculties of the third eye.

The Seventh Chakra: Realization

The energies operating here are extremely sensitive and delicate, of very fine frequency and requiring a high dosage of personal integrity, purity and harmlesness. If a person who does not possess these characteristics should stimulate this centre, he might feel as if he were being controlled or possessed.[6] Desiring power, subconscious forces eagerly grant him those powers for a price he can never really afford. Misuse of the faculties of this chakra echo faithlessness. The usurper constructs a fantasy world of his own desire.

This chakra rules the pineal gland, the upper brain and the right eye. It is directly connected to the buddhic web and through it to the monadic cell. It is fed by the second primary ray, the ray of wisdom. Interestingly, the pineal gland contains vestigial retinal tissue as well as a replica of each chakra – the pattern of the Total Man. It is the master control panel for the initiate.

When the individual's evolution brings him to this level, he truly gives birth to his Being, partaking of the sense of life's oneness. This centre represents integration with the Father-Mother totality, as the Son (Man) returns home. The Self understands that there are no limits to creation and that he is one with eternity. He has perfected a vehicle for conscious expression in the world. His individuated Self is unique but there are no attachments or identifications with this individuality which is offered in service. The entire monadic cell may express itself through this perfectly attuned, powerful and flexible, conscious personality. The perfect alchemist is born: the Man-God who lives and moves anonymously among humankind.

Normally chakras are operating on the frontal part of the body, at the level of entry of the light filaments from the rays. This means that the forces in operation express the horizontal projection-activity of the atom of consciousness in the world. The back or inner functions of the chakras do not awaken until the atom of consciousness is drawn inside the heart centre to activate the self-mastery attributes within the individual.

The first movement of consciousness, which is simultaneous on all chakras, is to relate out into the world in order to create an identity at personality levels. All the chakras are accessed and the personality acquires its experiences – its karmic entanglements – responding to and accentuating its own memory imprints. The energies and forces it uses are collectively engendered. Its body, its mind and its emotions are often desperate mechanisms of the collective subconscious. This is the path of identity formation where the person learns to shape and handle its personality.

The second movement is the descent journey. The first part was perceived in a sequential way that appeared to indicate an upward journey. We had not yet reached the stage of mastering the lower forces. The forging of lead into gold happens during the second part, when the person has acquired awareness at the level of the heart. This is where our human apprenticeship actually begins, through our varied relationships.

The process of redemption and karma-clearing begins, refining and defining the power and faculty at the level of elemental substance, in order to rise together with the kundalini force, in the definitive journey towards full consciousness. Only now does man possess enough real power and momentum to inherit the God-possibilities offered through mastery. This will be the third movement which expresses the real Human.

We receive energy from the rays through the chakras in inverse proportion to the quantity and quality of crystallization-adherences that we carry. If we can understand that we are living within an energy field filled with abilities, impressions and perceptions, and that this energy field is extremely sensitive to other vibrations of a like nature, we may begin to take better measures. We will know that every time our vibrations interact and resonate with others in the entire network of humanity, the lower frequencies exert a pull upon the higher ones, absorbing and disempowering them. If we treasure the still small voice within us, the tiny spark of true light within the heart, we might begin to care better for the kinds of friends and environments we place ourselves in, protecting and preserving the purity of our intent and life's precious materials. From the perspective of energy dynamics the picture is somewhat frightening. At the moment that we link up with someone in a relationship, even if it is not sexual, we open up the functions of the chakras in a horizontal way. We begin to form energetic circuits with them. We are pulled by them and they by us through the circuitry of the elemental forces. The only way to counterbalance this is to have an equal or stronger pull at the level of the heart within oneself.

As we develop heart-power and strive to live integrally we can simultaneously use the alchemical circuit alignment . This and other suggested protection exercises are a training measure meant to go hand in hand with honest self-appraisal.

Coincidentally there are natural everyday activities which can be included to develop and stabilize the activity of the individual chakras. It is important to stress here that sleep patterns should never be regulated, other than for obvious emergency requirements. This imposition creates a tension which is worse than any lack of sleep. When an individual begins to practice Inner Alchemy, or any consciousness inducing practices, his atom of consciousness begins to shift, creating a need for different amounts of rest, sleep, play and activity.

Here follow some grounding techniques for each of the chakras:

WAYS OF WORKING ON THE CHAKRAS

First Chakra:

- Pay closer attention to the body, being careful to redistribute awareness evenly, including that of weight and density.
- Take better notice of your skin in combination with the above, so as not to overtax the chakra, which responds strongly to cutaneous stimulation, but is also depleted from lack of it. Give this attention yourself.
- Lengthen the tolerance level by deepening it inside and throughout the organism.
- Place emphasis on the feet and in walking become aware of the sensation of the contact with the earth itself.
- Sense everything you touch with your whole body.
- Celebrate the body unit as a whole without separating it into parts.
- Train in practicality. Learn to balance your finances, including your cheque book.

Second Chakra:

Learn to distinguish between the mental activity that triggers emotion and the energy phenomenon of the emotion itself. Thinking as worry tends to aggravate the emotions. Become aware of emotions as an energy phenomenon rather than stressing the labelling of them.

- Spread and deepen the capacity to feel and discern emotional stimulus.
- Practise control over the emotions by consciously evoking them within yourself and without motivation. Learn to turn them on and off. Learn to focus and spread them alternately. Observe the quality of the energy in each one of them, and the effects each has over your mind and body.
- Learn to neutralize the energy generated by the emotions, through breathing methods and/or any of the practices suggested within the teaching of Inner Alchemy.
- Observe the effects of music on your feelings. Be sure to include some loud rock music, or music that you 'dislike' as well. Then neutralize.

- Practise giving without receiving: practise receiving without giving.
- Feel yourself as a responding entity. In other words, feel yourself feeling someone.
- Tune in to what people are feeling, consciously. Feel it in your body without attachments and then release it. Feel yourself as different from that.

Third Chakra:

- Practice saying yes to everything; practice saying no to everything. Note the effects. Sustain them.
- Experience submission and domination. Set this up in a conscious and integral way, preferably changing roles with someone who will experiment with you.
- Fortify the nervous system with appropriate exercise, soothing music and visualization practices. (The liquid golden light exercise provided later is good for this).
- Become aware of what you are desiring and how you are manipulating. Do this without inducing guilt.
- Stand on your own convictions.
- Reverse your fear mechanism.
- Save energy by making conscious movements and becoming aware of all movements that your body makes.
- Visualize a radiant sun in the solar plexus cavity and sustain that.
- Experience leading a group of people (children, especially).

Fourth Chakra:

- Become aware of your judgementalism. Note the dualism of all your likes and dislikes and practise changing that. For example, see how friends can become a hinderance (as a source of attachment), and how enemies can be a blessing (as a source of lessons).
- Practise giving something anonymously (without feeling virtuous).
- Visualize a huge golden sun within the chest. Irradiate consciously and regularly in your private meditation. Never aim your irradiation at anyone or at anything in particular. Let it illumine all about you equally. Sustain that.
- Learn to love the lower self, and all the lower forces within you unconditionally.
- Practise tolerance as an ability to neutralize negativity in the light chamber of the heart.

- Embrace – physically, mentally and emotionally.
- Create beauty in any and every way.
- Touch more people. Let the hands be the feelers of the heart.

Fifth Chakra:

- Listen to the sound of your own voice.
- Sing, chant, recite poetry and practise modulating the voice consciously (Exaggerate a little at first!).
- Imagine the frequency of the heart as a still, small voice within you. Listen to it.
- Sing lullabies to yourself, to plants, to animals…
- In meditation, enter into the silence as a presence without boundries
- Find your own resonant tone for each of the chakras in your body.

Sixth Chakra:

- Practise brain synchronization or whole brain exercises. These consist of stimulating each hemisphere individually and then both simultaneously. Try to hold two simultaneous images (one on each side). Two perceptions simultaneously.
- Consciously link-up your thinking to the heart frequencies by visualizing a flow between the heart and the third eye.
- Stop obsessively fretting about the future. Imagine that anything could happen tomorrow and accept that unknown factor.
- Be in this world and not of it simultaneously.
- Read abstract texts (philosopy or science or mathematics) regularly. Force yourself to think a little more abstractly each time.

Seventh Chakra:

- Consciously use your personality as an instrument, without preoccupation about what others think.
- Practise receiving the light that emanates from the Alchemical Circuit vertically; allow it to flow all the way down and through you.
- Be a ray of light

LIFE LESSONS AT THE LEVEL OF THE CHAKRAS

First Chakra

Purity. Responsibility for the use and care of the physical form and with the world of forms. Practicality and prosperity.

Second Chakra

The correct use of feeling and emotion. Reciprocity. Personal and social identity.

Third Chakra

The development and proper use of personal power. Ability to hold the peace. Personal control. Management and administration of energy. Co-operation and leadership. Impeccability.

Fourth Chakra

Tolerance. Discrimination and good judgment. Justice. Perception beyond duality. Unconditionality. True humanity.

Fifth Chakra

Correct use of will. Creativity. Correct use of sound frequencies. Learning to flow between the perception of infinity and time.

Sixth Chakra

Vision and intelligence. Concentration and consecration. Higher order. Correct mental projection.

Seventh Chakra

The awakening of the relationship between Man and God. Acceptance of personal meaninglessness; finding meaning in existence. Physical transmutation power. Cosmic Unity.

Chapter Five

ANATOMY OF POWER

The Power Behind Emotions

Love expresses itself in the highest levels of dimensional activity as pure effulgence, constant movement and generation. This same quality manifests in the human upper centres as one with power and intelligence, representing the driving force behind manifestation. In the lower triad, this energy as force provides us with an ability to generate and multiply, something we access continually through our emotions. Emotions generate energy and give birth to multiplicity; they magnify, multiply and amplify.

As the atom of consciousness activates the form aspect of the first chakra and moves through the second and third chakras, emotion as sensation is felt as pleasure or pain and becomes identified with the people and things perceived outside. This is how varieties of attachment and repulsion come into being.

The qualifications of energy and force as emotion create a certain amplitude and longitude, waves in fact, which fall into the category of harmonious or discordant, always linking the sender and his object. In this way emotions are the very motor power of relationships, and are present as an integral ingredient of life within all three lower chakras. Their centre of activity is the second chakra, although the power is derived from the third. The play of emotions is a true energetic dance of forces, as the people or things which these forces move are swayed, excited, lulled or dispersed.

The West has emphasized the development and understanding of both the second and third chakras' linear activity as psychology; the Orient has researched the spiritual and paranormal faculties of the navel as an agglutination point for the stocking of energy as force in the third dimension. It is up to us now to use the energetic wisdom of the Orient and the psychological expertise of Western technological thinking. Whereas the navel (also known as the 'hara') is basically a storage centre, a focus for vitality, the second and third chakras' dynamics shape human behaviour, particularly as it relates to karma.

The power of expression in an unenlightened person comes from his emotions. A more evolved individual serves himself of the 'hara' which is accessed through the intelligence of the heart chakra. The heart alone is unable to affect matter. In more conscious persons the 'hara' serves to shape matter and the 'bindu' acts upon etheric and higher substances which will produce a considerably higher circulatory and irradiatory activity.

Higher love as the essential alchemical ingredient emanates from the chamber of the heart without attachment or agitation. There is an awareness of reciprocity which has been termed 'empathy'. Crying often marks the passage of force from the solar plexus into the higher energetic frequencies which melt the forces much like ice becomes water when exposed to heat. The emotions themselves are distilled into the elixir of love. Emotions generate intensity or 'momentum', the force behind the quantum leap of consciousness. Emotional power can heal as it can also destroy.

A personalistic structure is the result of emotional force, or desire. This is how we become as we are. At first this is what our parents want, then what our friends want, then whatever the style of the times dictates. Only rarely is it what we consciously want. In the process of spiritual development, will, the essence of desire, is needed to direct energy. This will is focused desire as the intentionality of the third chakra.

Translated into will and aspiration emotional force accumulates into pure potency. Disciples and later Initiates use this to generate enough momentum to change levels of awareness, to deliberately alter the course of the atom of consciousness, to ignite the consciousness process itself, and ultimately to direct a variety of operations including the building of worlds.

Human emotions cover the gamma of human creation. Denser, more forceful emotions such as anger and rage reach destructive frequencies that deflect into resentment, disgust, annoyance, irritation and mild-dislike, while causing considerable disruption. Their frequencies belong to the involutionary forces which affect matter in ways that increase density and weight, and adversely attack the molecular structure of finer substances. Whenever negative emotions are released, they strengthen and increase the production of adherences.

Every time an ignorant, careless human being emits a negative emotion, he opens the door to the dark forces which plug into these emotions. In all too many cases it is a losing battle, setting up a momentum that only attracts more and coarser modalities. Furthermore, since like attracts like, the individual often attracts friends, partners psychology's forefathers have bequeathed us. This development cannot consist of more of the same thing. In other words, more theories and insights, including valid explanations about the irrational components of consciousness, although appealing naturally to the intellect can provide no more understanding than what we already have.

Psychology is the study of mind dynamics. In its highest correlate it is the study of Mind, that very same stuff that is the primal building block of creation. It provides us with essential training in the use of our natural resources, particularly our expansion of the concrete mind in grasping holistic and multidimensional concepts and ideations. It helps us learn grouping, association, cognition and relating consciously, teaching us the intricacies of forming, creating and embracing space and time, polarities, and the deep rhythms of the universe within and without us. It can take us to and beyond causality, through and beyond our personal history. I hope that these pages will provide experiential insight into the energetic relationship dynamics of the mind, body and emotions acting as one under a very real but undefinable focus of consciousness which seeks to merge with it.

The ordinary, unconscious human being portrays a veritable inferno of excitation and depression, alternately. The East has called this cyclic activity of cause and effect, the 'fruits of karma' and has observed it to manifest in six kinds of 'worlds' of human creation. In the Tibetan Buddhist map it is called 'the wheel of samsara'. This 'wheel' is the subject of innumerable books and 'tankas' (those colourful hangings that Tibetans are known for) and represents the worlds (or 'lokas') a man creates and participates of when his atom of consciousness is fixed in a certain pattern of emotional expression within the three lower centres. These worlds relate not so much to physical re-embodiment as to the continual cycle of death and rebirth within life itself, which creates a vicious circle. These six modalities lie within the three-dimensional range of experiences, inasmuch as they pertain to emotional and astral worlds of desire which underly the dynamics of relationship. The rotatory movement of the wheel of samsara could be interpreted as follows.

A person may temporarily live in a fairyland world of illusion and imagination, sustaining it as long as possible. This means as long as his whole vibrational range of frequency is able to sustain the higher voltage which accesses the upper astral layer of reality. The individual's personality structure at this level is usually poised around 'good', as opposed to 'bad' behaviour. This is the Deva World dictated by the ether element of consciousness.

In an almost rude awakening, the person may then find himself in a state of heavy stupor and unconsciousness out of which he can't seem to extricate himself. This is the result of the collapse of the vibrational level that he was artificially holding up, on the borrowed time and energy he had gained from his portion of good deeds. Here he feels stupid and apathetic, and is prone to his heaviest instincts. This is known as the World of Brute Consciousness and relates to the dynamics of the densest level of elemental forces. If he manages to wake himself up out of this level, he generates a proportionate level of intense emotional energy that launches him into the next level on the wheel.

The World of the Jealous Gods awaits him. Here the very feelings of passionate emotional activation produce in him jealousy and envy, possessiveness and greed which colour an intense curiosity for other worlds, particularly those he left behind. The suspicion which marks this stage is the negative expression of the air element of consciousness. This gives way to a kind of remorse which projects his awareness onto the following level.

Profound hunger and fear now dwell in him. His passions take on the form of ardent desire in a reality called the World of Hungry Ghosts, whose ruling component of consciousness is fire. This brings up a mild form of sobering, a very rudimentary form of humility which catalyses yet another level of reality.

The Human World, in Tibetan Buddhist terminology stands for the self-righteousness of egoism. The person begins to feel that he is indeed quite special and unique, puffed up by his own importance, through the negative aspects of the earth component of consciousness. His feelings are now marked by arrogance and intolerance. His mind is swarmed by doubts of all sorts which take him into the sixth world.

The Hell World and all the aggressions possible in a human being characterize this stage of reality, ruled by the water element of consciousness, which generates enough momentum to bring about relief through the polar opposite condition. He once again finds himself in the fairyland of his dreams and religious fervour. In this way he continues, caught up in the wheel of cause and effect, which is the meaning of samsara, or the everyday world.

I may easily have depicted the everyday life of most of humanity. Of course there are doors out of this wheel. These doors are the contrasting attributes of the positive emotions. Buddhist philosophy teaches us that equanimity and impartiality leads us out of the Deva World. Impeccability and integrity leads us out of the World of Brute Consciousness. A genuine sense of generosity, fraternity, and discernment coupled with a willingness to work lead out of the World of Jealous Gods. Discernment, discrimination and true perception lead out of the World of Hungry Ghosts. And acceptance, tolerance and understanding lead us out of the much cherished Human World.

1   There is always a feeling of rigidity. In the body this often manifests as the big-face syndrome. One is trapped behind a rather obvious face. The body too can become quite stiff. One finds it hard to laugh at oneself, for one takes oneself very seriously. Also there is an inability to do more than one thing at the time.

2   One feels 'noticed', either positively or negatively, since one happens to occupy quite a bit of space and take up people's time.

3   There is always some 'drama ' or another which involve people in many different ways. A common way is to agitate oneself and the environment by generating need and/or importance. Often one controls others (and hates them for it), or is controlled by others (and also hates them). The keynotes here are tragedy, danger and suffering.

4   Something always bothers or distracts one. Most often one distracts oneself sufficiently that one forgets to feel. (This is an especially difficult characteristic to spot oneself.)

5   There is always a battle or struggle going on somewhere. Everything is always complicated. One can't be direct or synthetic.

6   There is always a performance, a role to be played.

7   One is always anxious about being 'found out' and often projects this anxiety onto others and situations.

8   Someone or something else is always to blame. Maybe it is the weather, or the times, the planetary condition or your wife or mother.

9   There are always socially accepted excuses or justifications. One always does what is 'right' (if one is a 'goody-goody') or what is 'wrong' (if one is an alienated misfit, or a rebel).

10   One's behaviour always expresses extremes or excesses of some kind.

11   One is never silent or alone. There is always someone around, or failing that, there is always the internal dialogue.

12 One always needs props of some sort, notes, instructions, classes, etc (the 'can't-do-without' syndrome). This also manifests as a need to plan ahead and organise oneself. Inversely, one never seems to get it together to get organised.

13 One can't think or be in the present. Continuity is sought from the past or in the future.

14 One is afraid or just can't be oneself.

15 Before doing anything, one is swarmed by one's own opinions, which always act as a bucket of cold water.

16 There is always an enemy somewhere.

17 One 'invests' in people, things and situations and then complains about obligations and being 'tied' to others and to situations. One sets oneself up continually. On the other hand one is always afraid of losing something or someone.

18 One must defend one's image at all costs.

19 One is motivated by needs, all of which present great urgency.

20 One is all-aborbing oneself, always talking about oneself. Everything revolves around oneself.

21 There is always someone watching, even if it is the observer one has created in an effort to work on oneself.

Egoism always provides an always. Behaviour is polarized, with entire sets of characteristics opposing one another. Wherever there is a 'stupid' me there is also the 'bright' me. Wherever there is a 'proud' person, that person is also very 'humble'. When someone finds himself 'loving', chances are he can also be very 'hateful'. If he is 'insecure', he can also be 'confident and proud'. And the 'ambitious' individual is always secetly 'cowardly'. And on and on....

Before approaching the ways in which we can break the hold of our egoism and recognize the characteristics of the real personality, let's examine the underlying particularities which men and women individually possess by virtue of their gender.

These characteristics will determine female egoism and male egoism which, more than distinct traits, are ways in which each responds to the world and constructs their brand of selfishness.

Male and Female Personality

Men's physical polarity is positive. This means that the lowest centre expresses a positive charge. The second centre contains a negative polarity, while the third centre will again manifest a positive, active charge. The polarities of these three centres will underly the ways in which masculine psychology express itself in the world, with the heart centre presenting a great problem because of its negative positionality. The upper centres, when truly activated, or when expressing deviated lower forces, manifest positively at the level of the throat, negatively at the third eye, and finally positive at the uppermost centre on top of the head.

Positive and negative polarity refers to the ways in which the forces, or energies, affect behaviour, both psychological and spiritual. Positive refers to expressive modalities and negative reveals more receptive introspective processing. The negative activity absorbs and integrates within itself in order to influence expression at the next layer. These layers display concentrically (around the body core) what the chakras trigger through linear sequence along the body. If a man's second chakra has a negative charge at the level of physical expression, at the next layer, in his emotional body, he will express his emotions actively. This means that man's emotionality manifests in a more vulnerable inner way. His feelings on the emotional body level, rather than at the physical, are especially intense.

Looking at woman we see that her physical body is expressing a negative polarity. This allows her to absorb the positive male force inside her, which creates the atmosphere for the vehicle of the individual who will be the child. Her positive emotional polarization at the level of the second chakra bestows upon her an ability to physically and actively express feelings which sometimes overwhelm man's subtler emotional responses, bringing frustration upon her and confusion which, as anger, triggers off reactions in man's positive polarity at the solar plexus as excessive or abrasive rationality. Woman's solar plexus manifests negatively, which means that she does not have the same ability to deal with logic and objective thinking in the world, another source of misunderstanding which provokes unnecessary strife and competition between the sexes. Her emotional body however, 'knows' a lot more about itself than the male's. Woman's heart centre, in its positive modality, reflects her mind as intuition. This also provides woman with an enormous powerhouse which, if accessed correctly and at the proper time, can heal and bring positive forces into physical manifestation all around her.

At the level of the upper bodies, woman's throat centre accesses more subtle inner modalities than man, while her third eye, the visionary and higher intuitional centre, is again powerfully charged with positive polarity. Her uppermost centre, that which connects her with monadic impulse, is negatively charged, linking her strongly and absorbingly to electronic receptivity.

Here follows a chart depicting the polarities of the chakras in men and women, and the polarity of the bodies (or layers) of vibrational activity surrounding the physical.

POLARITIES IN MAN AND WOMAN

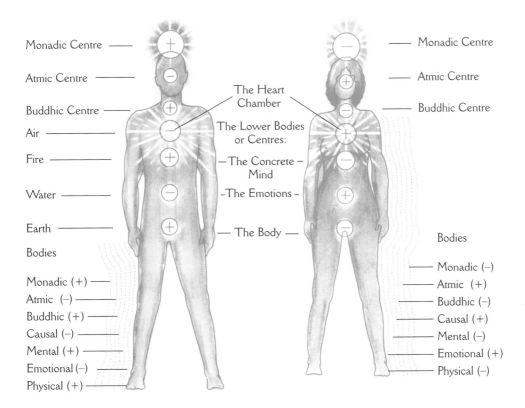

Man		Woman
Monadic Centre — (+)		(−) — Monadic Centre
Atmic Centre — (−)		(+) — Atmic Centre
Buddhic Centre — (+)	The Heart Chamber	(−) — Buddhic Centre
Air — (−)	The Lower Bodies or Centres:	(+)
Fire — (+)	—The Concrete Mind	(−)
Water — (−)	—The Emotions—	(+)
Earth — (+)	— The Body —	(−)

Bodies

Monadic (+)	Bodies
Atmic (−)	Monadic (−)
Buddhic (+)	Atmic (+)
Causal (−)	Buddhic (−)
Mental (+)	Causal (+)
Emotional (−)	Mental (−)
Physical (+)	Emotional (+)
	Physical (−)

If we consider these positive and negative charges seriously, we gain a deep under-standing of female and male behaviour, including the needs which manifest differently in their personalities. Taking the physical modality first, we can see how men are innately more physical and this physicality will express itself concretely on the physical, mental and even in the emotional plane. This physicality means tangibility and action. As woman's physical pole is negative, she does not naturally place so much emphasis on physical expressions unless they are motivated by emotional dynamics, which is her strong positive pole in the lower centres. In the world, as power and intellectuality, men definitely have the upper hand, but their dependence upon women at the level of the emotions and heart centre makes them especially vulnerable.

It is difficult for women to compete with, or gain understanding from men who express dynamic linear modalities. Because of these, and other deep rooted differ-ences, women seldom stabilize at the heart centre in order to access consciousness, remaining all too often at the level of emotionally tinged spirituality. And unless woman reaches the level of the heart, the evolution of humanity as a whole will remain mediocre. Only correct and positively polarized heart energy can catalyse the alchemy of the lower bodies. This places a great responsability upon women and upon humanity to see that woman gets there. For this reason, up to now spirituality has been relegated to the domain of the subtle bodies, expressing predominantly mental activity. At the mental level, of course, males are dominant, bringing with that the dangers of intellectualism devoid of emotional depth.

The impact of perfect consciousness within a male physical expression implies the positive spread of this frequency unto the body of humanity, manifesting the energies of the monadic ray positively, which explains why there have been so many more male masters in the past. As the need for these times is the transmutation of sub-stance itself (heart activity), in grounded, active spirituality, the greater number of teachers may be found among women themselves through the spiritual influence of therapy and in the fields of education, politics, science and even finance.

The composite picture of ordinary man and woman, has been well described by Torkom Saradayan in 'Woman: The Torchbearer of the Future'. Woman's mind expresses language emotionally. She sees everything through her emotions, identify-ing herself with what she sees. From this her possessive attitude in expressions such as, 'my son', 'my husband', and the like. If she does not evolve her emotional attach-ment, she becomes egocentric. morbid and demanding. Her main weapon is to attack the instinctual nature of man and to condemn his physicality in an attempt to control him. She unconsciously calls attention to herself. Unable to control her emo-tions she projects them continuously and then lies to herself.

The composite picture of ordinary man is not any nicer. Through unconscious programming, man's language is preferentially concrete. He knows how to use his mind well, without the emotional disturbances that cloud woman's rationality, mastering linear and geometric modalities and translating emotions into concepts. This turns him into a cold, calculatingly cerebral, distant and unreal person. He thinks he is contemplating reality whereas he in fact replaces it with his ideas about it. He attacks woman's emotions and belittles her, or else he raises her onto an unreal pedestal (from where she will undoubtedly fall), in order to conquer her. All the time he uses his mind to exploit her.

The viciousness that manifests in associations between members of the same sex is just as dismal, fostering suspicion, doubt, competition and possessiveness, alienation, aloneness, isolationism, pretence and superficiality.

The essential differences between the sexes are meant to support and foster growth for one another in companionship and friendship. Once the heart has been accessed in man or in woman, the personality differences, that is the psychological polarities of the lower bodies, cease to have a compulsively dominant influence. Both sexes become both male and female in spirit – two-in-one – while their bio-physical expression in their bodies continues to irradiate their gender in refined perfection. An enlightened man will be deeply and emotionally responsive; an enlightened woman will be clear, intelligent and discerning. The focus of integrated activity is at the heart, into which all three lower attributes have been assimilated.

The most important task that faces us worldwide is to understand the distinctly different characteristics and abilities of the genders. The next task is to set right the imbalances created by the deviated faculties of the first and third chakras, and the confusion added to this at the level of the chaotic forces of the second centre. The positive male polarities of the first and third chakras express the negative materialistic characteristics of the centres, while the positive female second chakra magnifies the negative indulgencies of emotional excess.

The worldwide picture is the following:

First Chakra: The positive polarity expresses urgency and violence, excessive emphasis on sensation and selfish gratification, the use of people and natural resources for exploitation.　　　　(men)

The negative polarity manifests a lack of grounding, a negation of body consciousness, fear, insecurity and lack of personal resources, poverty and old age.　　　　(women)

Second Chakra: The positive polarity expresses emotional manipulativeness
and irrationality, seductiveness and attachment, possessiveness and guilt, and all forms of emotional excesses. (women)
The negative polarity manifests a lack of feeling, dry, brittle
superficiality, lack of warmth and emotional responsiveness. (men)

Third Chakra: The positive polarity expresses ambition and obsession with
power, exploitation and manipulativeness. (men)
The negative polarity manifests dependency upon outer
authority and discipline as well as an avoidance of it, no true
knowledge of self or ability to control the self. Rampant fear
of power and a masochistic attraction to being dominated. (women)

The icing on the rather sour cake is the little heart centre which, with such poor
backing, manifests opinionated intelligence on the one hand and airy-fairy wooly
thinking on the other.

Transcendence

What is it not to be in egoism? What allows some people to slip out of it more easily
than others? Are there any dangers to living without it?

Having defined egoism as a composite of standard sex polarization, cultural trends
set by the times, and chakra qualities in manifestation, we now face the almost
humanly impossible task of stepping out of it... if we can. By stepping out of it I mean
being aware and in control, without becoming obsessed or driven by it. In simple
terms, not to be influenced by its justfications, so that we can perceive and function
from a higher vantage point, one that is inclusive and truly human. The symbolic, primal, essential battle between egoism and transcendence marks the process of consciousness, transmutation and redemption of matter. It is fought between the sexes. It
is fought between East and West. It occurs within the self. The only hope lies in
making that quantum leap within the innermost recesses of the individual self.

The real 'I' as a presence has to be present, not as a running commentator or as
an urgent need, but as an aware and active consciousness. This is achieved gradually.
There may be occasional relief through dips into a delicious silence that is immensely pleasurable and fulfilling. There may be longer periods of time spent in a state of
altered consciousness, a kind of wonderful no-where. Yet we always come back to

find the mechanism that operates the personality and its egoism intact. There will be hurdles, in making both mind and body flexible. As we come to recognize our attachment and accept the vantage point of a presence within a flexible personality, we can enter into the silence more easily and nourish ourself.

There is no continuity other than what we lend to things. At the best of times, we will find that 'I' is a result of the moment dictated by the need of that moment. That state of presence reflects the greater Presence within us all. It is our real link with humanity. Only if we are nourished in this way can we have the appropriate charge of available energy to help anyone. Once the body, mind and emotions are in the same time-place, the space that emerges in the now is the experience of being real, of being oneself.

The referential must be switched from the control of mind into the modality of the heart, from thoughts, ideas and linear terminologies to concentric experiential references, yet simultaneously keeping and ability to use, as in the case of the personality itself, the linear modalities of operation in the world.

Although this process is individual, there is a powerful force which is engendered when two whole people come together in relationship. This is especially potent between members of the opposite sex. From it will arise the Real Man of the future.

The Real Personality

The real personality is a function of the moment. It is an arrangement that rearranges itself according to changing situations, never automatic or predicated on habit or routine. It is built upon and uses the personality as consciousness itself. We become a presence.

1   The point of reference is transferred to the state of being present as an experience rather than an identity.

2   There is tremendous flexibility which allows one to flow within many possible modalities, or identities. Often there is atypical behaviour.

3   Without a set structure, there is greater spontaneity, marked by unpredictability rather than by assessment or inner compulsion.

4   It lives without conventional meanings. The meaning is in one's own existence.

5   It is an energy phenomenon from which higher intelligence irradiates naturally. It also and simultaneously expresses vitality and feels vitally alive.

6   It is a let-go. It enjoys itself without tension. There is a sense of joy and freedom.

7   It feels very ordinary. It doesn't have investments to defend or protect. It acts, lives, thinks and speaks simply.

8   It laughs at itself and doesn't take itself seriously. It plays itself and knows how to use the personality consciously.

9   It responds humanly to people and situations, neither emotionally involving itself nor projecting indifference. It doesn't care what others think, and yet is not callous or insensitive.

10   It likes adventure and risk-taking without being careless or reckless.

11   It is humble without showiness. It likes itself.

12   It accepts situations it cannot change without arguments or resistance.

Some Ways of 'getting there': Antidotes

1   Playing oneself.

2   Playing another (as in acting).

3   Letting go.

4   Changing the habits of behaviour: walking, talking, sitting and doing different (atypical) things; trying on different attitudes and different expressions.

5   Laughing at oneself.

6   Pretending to know exactly what's going on without explanations and acting from that knowingness.

Chapter Six

RELATIONSHIP DYNAMICS

Karma and Relationship

What usually draws one person to another is loneliness, not awareness. The ideal of relationship awakens the desire of sometime finding understanding and fulfilment. The idealized person satisfies a yearning, often like a desperate hope covering the fear of aloneness. This is why so many relationships lead to sorrow and disillusionment. There is no way that another can fill us up or quench the thirst for an experience which may not be ours to have.

We relate with another for the same reasons which hold us onto life, to prove ourselves to ourselves. In this way friendships, enmities, business associations, love relationships and even parenthood are founded upon a common dynamic: they are mirrors. Our relationships reflect all our traits. And yet each one also offers a new hope.

In the world, love manifests as physical, emotional, and mental attraction and operates within two aspects of the same physical law of polarity: (1) as the psychological interface and circulation of energies in ordinary relating, and (2) as the exchange of vital fluids and substance in the couple relationship. Most people make a distinction between normal relations in the world and 'love' relationships. In reality their dynamics are identical. In this book the difference is seen as one of degree and scope of irradiatory influence only. Obviously, the second kind is stronger and produces a more powerful impact upon our material world.

Relationships, particularly man-woman love relationships are the quintessence of life's spice. We only need to tune into the radio in any country of the world, to plug into the sweet dream – the uncertainty and the hope, the chase and the conquest, the pleasure and the hope of greater joy...! He or she will 'always' be there. He or she will 'hold your hand' ...forever! All problems melt away by meeting our prince charming or fairy princess. It is a wonderful stage of enchantment... and we wish it might last forever. Even old folk smile and fantasize... The dream never really came true. It never really does. It is a sweet-sweet dream and many of us know it all too well. Yet we choose to forget. We choose to dream on.

Although this chapter deals mostly with the dynamic of relationships between members of the opposite sex, it also applies to any individual who is involved with another person in the 'leela' of creation. Energetic circulation within the body operates identically within both sexes regardless of circumstance.

Oriental esoteric tradition breaks energy down into different types. The kind which forms the core of sexual relationships is what Chinese Taoists call 'ching' and Indian Tantrikas call 'shakti'; I call it bio-physical or vital energy. This particular kind of energy acts as force with the power and denser consistency of the elements. It is very different from subtle forms of grace, for example, although optimally it will also lead there. The purpose of spiritual work is to derive benefits from that denser substance while also refining it into a finer force where it may be used to run our body and our life in accordance with higher principle.

In this book this process represents the human alchemy which is necessary for the development of consciousness. This implies examining the effects produced by our mis-management of substance and force: our relationships. The really conscious individual flows with life and with the situations that life presents us with.

At this point in our reading we may have assessed our management of the three lower centres well enough to know the extent of our karmic load – in other words our degree of neediness, laziness, urgency, indifference, and defiance or avoidance of relationships in general. We have begun to look at what obstructs or drives the course of our relating in the world. We may even have perceived the joke behind the problems encountered in relationships, regardless of how different and unique we may consider them. Our reactions are standard and rather robotic. We may notice that relationship 'problems' are always the same: one rigid personality fighting with another rigid personality. Our relationships may be a living hell. Or maybe they are a living death.

So, 'Why are we together?', we might ask.

Let's examine some of the reasons that have been given to me in my workshops:

1   I can't live without him (or her). Life holds no meaning without him (or her).

This person has not been able to assume responsibility for his energy or identity and has projected the meaning for his/her life onto the partner. It would be good to review the pages for the first and second chakra obsessions.

2   He (or she) makes me feel good.

This is all too often spoken from the perspective of physical addiction or emotional neediness. In some cases it is a subtle sado-masochistic dynamic that empowers or dis-empowers each in a game of projection that keeps the melodrama interesting. There usually is an under current of energetic vampirism with narcissist overtones.

3   He (or she) is a good man (or woman).

This can be a healing friendship and can also read 'good father', or 'good mother'. If one is married to the good father or good mother figure, one most probably received the approval of society, if not of one's own parents. These relationships usually hold little sexual intensity and are rather boring for the person who holds this view. It may have been an excellent choice for security and to keep one from feeling oneself deeply at the mature level of sexuality. There is usually some other projection going on as well: the other is the good one and you are guilty but grateful.

4   I like to be with him (her).

Please examine why and what for. If you find that you can be equally well on your own, and you manage to stay aware and independent, then your relationship stands a chance.

Now to the more 'poetic' and 'mystical' reasons...

5   Fate brought us together. It just 'happened'.

Things just don't happen. One is constantly sending out calls (usually unconsciously) to attract that which one wants, that which one is avoiding, or that which one has become, which describe the three kinds of karmic relating. This statement reveals a certain amount of irresponsibility on the part of the individual who thinks like this.

6   He (or she) is my true soulmate... or ...my twin soul!

True what?! If this person were your soulmate or twin soul, you probably wouldn't be able to tolerate his (or her) proximity or the voltages which arise from such a meet-ing! A twin soul is an entity belonging to the same monadic cell as the individual. It is the same life-source that animates both. These entities rarely meet, save in cases like that of Francis of Assisi and Saint Claire, or that of Teresa de Avila and Juan de la Cruz. These meetings are never for sexual exploitation. When and if there is a meeting, and a recognition, which already requires a good deal of consciousness, the beings are at such an exalted level that they would never even think such things. The meeting is strictly for monadic purposes, to serve greater humanity. Please don't fantasize about this further.

7   He (or she) is beautiful!

It may be true, but what is this person doing with that? This rings of idolatry. It sounds to me like there is a pedestal somewhere and some misplaced devotion.

8   I like his (or her) 'energy'.

This usually means sexual energy. Whereas there certainly is nothing wrong with that, in most cases it is the only reason. Even if the person involved claims to like their 'heart' energy, it is most often projected sexual compulsion, embellished and covered with chocolate syrup. It's pure and simple sexual exploitation.

9.   I don't know...

No comment.

The truth about karmic relationships, which are usually any kind of relationship, is that they dramatically portray lessons at the level of the lower chakras which the individual has not completed. One day one of the partners may wake up to the truth, that he or she is projecting authority, power, satisfaction, or anything else outside of himself, and choose to get out of it. Herein lies the greatest test that his own higher conscience might give him: how to do this with integrity.

In most cases, 'when the going gets rough the rough get going'. The primary reason for divorce is the discovery of compulsive or obsessional attachments, which include the dutiful ones as well. The individual is confronted with his own ugliness. Rather than facing it within himself, he might continue to project it outwardly, blaming, accusing, insulting or humiliating his once dearly-beloved. In such strife he leaves the partner, to find another 'better' person. Many times this new person will present the same dilemma and he might again divorce... and remarry... and divorce ad nauseam. And in cases where he does find this 'better' person who stays a 'better' person in his or her view, it is usually because this 'better' person doesn't present any challenges. He, or she tucks him comfortably into 'beddy-bye' and puts him to sleep 'nicey-dicey'.

Now, what about the sincere person who discovers that he is in a committment with someone who can no longer 'play' with him? The first step this person might take, is to try to help his partner recognize what is happening. This must be done artfully, delicately, sensitively, and with a great deal of patience which will forge the moulding of his own character. After having done his best, and this means without suffering, loading himself with guilt, or escaping into a lover on the side, – if it is possible in the circumstances – this person might choose to separate. This can only happen when the individual has in his own estimation acted integrally.

There are many good justifications for the individual who finds life intolerable in the home and seeks the comfort of a relationship outside of marriage. The best ones usually point to the fragile health of the partner, to the supposed 'needs' of the children, and to the unstable or risky financial situation. I can't help seeing how the person set it all up. Diverting his attention, soothing himself and ultimately dividing himself between two relationships is not the answer. I smell cowardliness somewhere, disguised as concern or just plain fear of being alone. I am amazed at the number of people who are rotting within marriages that lead nowhere because they fear leaving their nests. There is no way to side with anyone. One is exactly where one needs to be and the way in which one deals with this is the index of consciousness.

If the karmic lesson involved was not resolved for the individual who was left behind, he/she will no doubt and very quickly find another person with whom to play out their neurosis... until and if they eventually wake up. Some may choose to play the victim role a little longer, sending all kinds of hooks to the old partner. As long as these antics hook into the other, the game goes on.

Karmic lessons are resolved within the individual himself. There is no such thing as having to complete the lesson with one person exclusively. There is no excuse for torture. A lesson is integrated within one's self. If the other person is not cognizant of the need for change, then they must play their needs out with someone else. By the same token, one never escapes consequences. If one doesn't learn under the present conditions, next time the lesson comes unexpectedly with more impact. Karmic force resonates two similar vibrations only; the lesson is in the handling of that vibration and does not tie anyone to another person.

We must not forget that in learning to handle, say, the forces of the second chakra, in our ignorance, enthusiasm, or through our own negativity, we involved many people with our emotions. Particularly during adolescence and the heat of early adulthood we attract friends and lovers using physical and emotional seduction, all the while delighting in the game and 'breaking hearts'.

The greatest karmic ties however seem to be created learning to handle the personal power forces of the third chakra. We become involved or involve others in the games of control and victimization. In Latin cultures particularly, where man's domination over women is the expected norm, women project unto their men the figure of authority, and with that all the power to control them. He projects onto her the role of his mother, usually going elsewhere to meet the lover he cannot find in the wife. Women who suddenly become 'spiritualized' and can no longer tolerate what they now consider the 'grossness' of sexuality, use their newly-defined spiritual identity as a weapon for revenge on the one hand and escapism on the other. Handling, projecting or withstanding violence, we come to inflict and suffer many incidents of emotional and mental violation.

There is also karma by omission, the times we didn't stand up for ourselves, or the times that echo the defence statement of the Nazi war criminals: 'I was just following orders!'. Or, 'I didn't know what I was doing'. How many mothers stand by letting their husbands abuse their children? How many husbands blinded by their sexual addiction, ignore the plea of their children? How many men look the other way when their wife betrays them, preferring to lie to themselves instead of losing her. It is important to understand that not committing an act makes us an accessory to that act.

Honestly answer the following questions silently:

1   What are the reasons behind my relationships? (Examine each reason and each kind of relationship.)

2   What have I learned or am learning with each one? Or inversely, what lessons am I avoiding.

3   What contracts have I entered into? What are the conditions? Please note here that many relationships between friends and lovers are contractual and conditional. Examine your price.

4   What creates confusion and entanglement in my relationships? What is it that clashes or creates tension... in me... or in others through me? (In other words how do others tend to see you).

5   Which are the difficult situations or relationships in my life? (Examine the under-lying dynamics to find out why, and how they could be turned around.)

6   Which are the easier relationships in my life? (Ibid.)

7   Which are the negative patterns within the difficult relationships that need to be transmuted? This will include violence in the physical sense, intense, emotionally triggering liasons, and situations in which there is a history of compulsion, lack of control, resentment, abandonment, giving-up or giving-in, energetic vampirism, power plays or implicit threats or in some way fear, or anger, control or domi-nation.

Here follows a chart that illustrates different types of relationships when the unit res-onates with the frequency of a particular centre.

First Chakra	Compulsive sexuality, animal instinct, sensation at cutaneous levels. Physical sado-masochism. Sexual exploitation. Lesson: Purity; sacramental ritualism.
Second Chakra	Psychological sex, eroticism and sensuality. Mirroring and projection. Father-Mother impressions. Intensity and identifi-cation. Lesson: Discrimination and discernment; joy and abil-ity to play.
Third Chakra	Power plays, domination, punishment, control and manipula-tion. Attraction to symbols of power such as money and poli-tics. Levels of glamour and illusion. Lesson: Detachment and strength of character; vitality and independence.
Fourth Chakra	Empathy and sympathy. Lesson: Fidelity and synthesis.
Fifth Chakra	Simultaneity and reciprocity. Lesson: Truth and light.
Sixth Chakra	Vision and intelligence at the level of the higher mental body
Seventh Chakra	True spiritual contact.

As we examine ourself, it should be without guilt. It is no longer in style to suffer martyrdom, or to promote a persecution campaign. When we spot our or another's faults we should look upon them with detachment. If compassion is not yet possible, then humility must be attempted. Feeling 'bad' is just another face of egoism.

Consider the 'good' karmic attachments with equal impartiality. The companionship, the help, the inspiration received... We are basically terrified of liberating ourselves (and the others) from them, believing that we stand to lose the love or friendships which these relationships provide. We don't stop to consider that what we might discover is another being altogether, a separate reality which inspires our own wholeness.

When one is in the flexible-personality modality one does not need another or need to be needed, which is a typical syndrome of emotional addiction. The fullness discovered in meeting and interacting with another whole and liberated individual is magnificent. One can be together and alone simultaneously. The freedom and spaciousness experienced is the greatest gift of love that can be given or received. In order to arrive at that state, take courage to uncover the needy child inside who still wants mommy and daddy, guidance, comfort, protection, or power. Let us consider the price we pay in order to get these things. In other words, why we sell ourselves and how we buy others.

Common Relationship Patterns

Relationships between persons who vibrate at the level of the lower centres create behaviour patterns of three types: sexual love, emotional love and competitive love. These behaviour patterns are set by the circulation of energy along certain paths within the three lower centres, intensifying the heavy or negative qualifications of the centres.

When two persons are tied in a relationship at any of the three expressions of karmic attraction and repulsion, each of the partners resonates a chord within the other's corresponding centre, causing the filaments of light to literally weld together into chain-like formations. These chains serve to transmit trigger-like reactions rather than conscious responses. With time this becomes crystallized into compulsions. I will give a few examples.

A man and woman tied at the level of physical carnality or sexual love will experience constant craving for the presence (or thought) of the other. The horizontal link conducts their sexual force primarily within the first centre. This kind of love is often projected onto one of the body parts, as in the case of the foot-fetishist. In some cultures the idol is the breasts, or the buttocks, the legs, or the face. Usually the object of this kind of affection is a part of the anatomy and not the person itself. In many cases not even this type of affection is present.

The circuit dwells at the grossest level of excitation. The sexual act, while intensely passionate, does not last very long unless the persons have recourse to technique, which at this stage is invariably used without sensitivity or consciousness. Without technique the frequency of sexual intercourse makes up for the brevity. There is tremendous mental excitement and often an imbalance at the hormonal level which exacerbates excitation. Sexual talk adds to the stimulation of the cutaneous portions of the body, called the erogenous zones. The primitive bent of the mind serves to activate and hold the atom of consciousness outside and in front at the level of local stimulation, amplifying sensation with pornographic imagery, language, music, foods or drugs. This is the sex of the masses and the technocrats.

It is important to understand that at the level of the lower chakras the triggering mechanism always implies mental activity, tuning into collective subconscious thoughtforms instead of within the feeling sanctity of the organism as nature would dictate. The sensation is registered inside the body, although in fact the phenomenon is externally produced. This fosters enslavement.

Moving only slightly up the scale of complexity we come to the excitement produced at the level of emotional love. Contractual friendship falls into this category. Need is now projected onto the personality rather than the physical body of the other to gratify the indwelling longing to feel protected and taken care of. Here we often find the mass of middle-class humanity, those whose strictly physical needs may not be so important. There is usually a disconnection from the body proper in favour of the emotions, which have been starved, repressed or over-emphasized. As most emotional needs are mentally sustained, temporary satisfaction is found through the mental imput of the other in vows and promises of some sort. Security is achieved through status symbols or the physical presence of the other. These persons can't do anything alone and most often can't live apart. In the case of couples, living together may be a hell of fear, insecurity, jealousy and possessiveness experienced internally within the marriage or by the unit against outsiders.

Examples of this sort of relationship abound. The husband provides money, comfort, and tangible objects which represent emotional security. The wife reciprocates with food, the means through which she usually proves herself a good wife. Together they constitute rather harmless and contented bellies leading somewhat boring lives. They usually not only identify but side with one another against imagined dangers from the outside world, forming strong alliances of prejudice and fanaticism. Their habits support and feed their paranoia. The intensity of their emotional addictions strengthens the bond between them. This kind of bonding is frequently seen in ideological or spiritual groups and professional clubs as well.

Food and status often replace sexual gratification but not always. In some cases there may be real arousal when one of the partners plays upon the emotions of the other. There is much manipulation. A favourite game played is 'catch-me-if-you-can'. Excitement is provoked by the chase. The triggering emotions usually imply danger, which produces a kind of suffering that ignites a rudimentary form of affection, or remorse, that translates as excitement. This threat, although focussed upon the second centre, carries overtones of the first centre, where the survival mechanism recalls violence.

At the third level, competitive love is marked by a system of reward and punishment. Ongoing conflict of interests and opinions colours this level with antagonism, competition and mental blackmail. By sheer force of will the other is conquered. There is continual defiance evoking passionate intensity in both conqueror and conquered. After a battle of wills the victor may turn to the victim intending to make peace, only to be met with rejection. This excites him (or her) further into more anger and indignation. This can go on for a very long time.

There is always the hope that the other will recognize one's 'worth'. In these relationships a great deal of importance is placed upon being right. This peculiarity resonates in the outside world where the persons usually seek power and prestige as a replacement for the organic fulfilment which their volatile lovemaking fails to produce. These couples argue a lot and nit-pick constantly, using reward and punishment as a way of expressing love for one another.

There is no way out of these relationships unless one of the partners recognizes the automatic mechanism that runs their lives. Even when both partners become aware of these patterns it is very difficult to dissolve the thoughtforms, (or chains) created to redirect the energies. The undoing process is difficult and painful, requiring tremendous courage and humility in facing up to one's own self and the projections which have absorbed another. There is no use in blaming the other person.

Partners need to work on redirecting their behaviour in order to repolarize the relationship which has become tinged with discord, creating very real and often tangible negative energy fields around the auras. The loss of sexual interest which results is often a consequence of the loss of polarity between the partners as the energies become welded into each other.

We need to preserve the sense of difference and respect for personal space, in order to sustain natural attraction as energy play. Even good people can fall into the rut of boredom and irritation caused by insistent proximity. Although most people object to this, I wholeheartedly recommend separate bedrooms for couples. Lacking this, I suggest the practice of some kind of ritual which will repeatedly remind the partners of their difference and individuality.

There is little positive effect from these kinds of energy circulation aside from the illusory gratification and often smugness of the participants tied by this kind of love-hate competition and ambitiousness which often infiltrates into business circles and the communications and education fields. All too often people are puppets of the collective subconscious. Relationship at any of the three lower levels leads to a loss of vital energy. At the first centre the loss is direct and immediate, as there is no real circulation to speak of. Each person is locked in self-gratification within himself. The vital force is spilled and returns immediately to the collective planetary pool without being positively qualified. On the contrary, it is often polluted by the human thoughtforms evoked during intercourse. At the second centre, vital force is coloured by the emotional qualifications of the individuals.

There is unfortunately only a slight possibility of the individuals generating positive emotions and establishing an impeccable code of ethics which could raise the relationship to the level of the heart. In harmony, which is the word used by Taoists for love, we can feel tremendous affinity with another. This usually goes hand-in-hand with a clear appraisal of differences, including the other's faults. These relationships are not characterized by conflict, tension or excitement, but embody joy, poise, stillness, awareness and genuine challenge as opposed to defiance. The parties involved stand a chance of maintaining a separation of identity while merging energetically to catalyze higher consciousness.

It is difficult to maintain a proper perspective in a society where 'we-ness', conformity and mediocrity is the norm, and where the other is a projected self. In relationships where higher levels of attunement are present, the modality of the heart is able to grow and nourish the entire bio-physical and psychological equipment, without there being an investment to defend or a private bliss to protect. This resonance spills over and into the environment and the home, fostering creativity and professional fulfilment. Instead of always saying 'we want...', or 'we think...', mature persons are able to express themselves directly and individually, acknowledging themselves and their freedom of choice. Coming together does not imply a glueing together of identities or a battle for survival.

Rather than being filtered or triggered by mental or emotional collective mechanisms, the body itself responds organically and wholly to life with its individual rhythms and cycles of activity and repose. A vibrant, healthy, self-aroused and synchronized organism responds in autonomous ways to polarities, and challenging differences, only now the vitality sensed is directed by conscious intelligence seated upon choice and appropriateness.

Consciousness is no longer susceptible to manipulation from collective thought-forms although it may perceive and sense them. Behaviour is no longer compulsive. An open and conscious individual feels intensely but he responds rather than reacts to his environment. Such an individual, properly grounded in his or her body can serve to trigger positive modalities in the partner, including reversals.

For woman, spiritual polarization is even more significantly instrumental. Her positive polarity at the level of the second centre serves as a bridge with her positive pole at the heart. The spiritualization of a relationship, the upliftment of the male's energy and the inspiration of the progeny is largely conditioned by the consciousness of the woman. A very positive vibration is irradiated within the heart chakra that can literally give birth to spiritual consciousness by catalysis.

Whereas many men achieve alone, it is a far easier and faster process if the man is aided and inspired by feminine energy. Ordinary man cannot raise his vibratory frequency beyond the mental and into the higher centres without this polarity. Nor can he attain to the transmutation of his base energy in order to affect cellular transmutation without the positive input of the female heart.

When a woman is not awakened at the level of the heart, no matter how spiritually conscious a man might be, the energy will most often not rise to the place where transmutation can occur. Man's higher energies, while vitally serving to trigger woman's higher intuition, would need also to ignite an opening at the level of the consciousness of the heart before as a couple they can both reach higher vibrational frequencies. Woman triggers this quantuum leap in man directly as positive emotional nourishment.

Energy Circulation within the Couple Relationship:

In sexual relationships, energy flows out through the male positive pole to enter the female negative pole. This immediately feeds into her emotional positive polarity at the second centre. Unless she is a rather limp specimen, she returns the energy directly through the first or second centre. If he is a potent male he will sustain the circulation of sexual force as long as she returns it. The kind of affection between them fuels the sexual link between them, which provides the base for every kind of circulation including the higher ones, particularly if the emotions are kept at the positive range. When the emotions or other second intentions are not constructive, the energy will fall into any one of the combinations which create the three lower modalities of behaviour. The interplay between psychological and vitality flow will be conditioned by the degree of individual personality integration.

In a positive sexual relationship the circulation, always dependent upon the base potency, may continue to weave through the other passages created between sympathetic centres, gathering more and more momentum; and especially upon receiving the impact of light activity at the heart it can journey upwards and onwards towards organic and spiritual fulfilment.

Although not all relationships are fed by vital sexual potency, relationships may journey together with gathered and increasing spiritual intensity through energy passages formed between and within the subtle bodies. In this manner we can see that organic and spiritual fulfilment are neither mutually exclusive nor dependent. They, in fact, usually happen separately. Yet, in order to affect the evolution of matter positively, they must be seen as two facets of the same phenomenon.

When the energy of a relationship reaches the level of the heart between members of opposite polarity, vital energy circulation can only be sustained if the negative polarity at the heart (in this case the male) opens to receive the charge at physical, emotional and mental levels. Whereas he may be able to maintain a physical momentum going, woman's subtle satisfaction will not be attained unless he absorbs that positive charge at all levels including the heart. Lacking this, woman will perceive it intuitively, although she may not always be able to interpret it verbally. Such a relationship is spiritually doomed to stagnate, and causes frustration on many levels.

When a male receives the energy on all levels, he can rise into higher consciousness by allowing himself to experience profound vulnerability. In this case he will acquire respect and appreciation for the woman. His own sense of himself will undergo deep transformation and softening. But not every male is open to this kind of deep humbling experience which shatters the male personality, and all too often, particularly in male-oriented cultures where 'macho'-like behaviour is stressed, he will attempt to dominate the woman by imposing his aggressive solar plexus modality.

When the male lacks either physical potency or impeccability, he will fall into passive submission, progressively losing the woman's respect and his own sense of self-worth. In some cases the impact of the woman's heart energy will cause a collapse of his energy. He may even fall asleep (literally)!

As woman surrenders to man on the physical level, man surrenders to woman at the level of the heart. Real power, in the spiritual sense, is transferred to the male at the heart. He must then rise into his new position of real power and dominance. A spiritually awakened woman recognizes this only too gladly. In this way 'real' men and 'real' women are born. Unfortunately we see far too many henpecked husbands, tyrants, 'macho' He-men, aggressive, irritable women, and frustrated lackeys around.

Within the dynamic at the heart centre lies the great secret that forever ends the battle of the sexes: the art of regaining strength within vulnerability. Where reverence, respect and courage are cultivated instead of weakness, escapism and denigration, there is true happiness and fulfilment. This fulfilment is not just sexual gratification; it includes the psychological and spiritual counterpart of the energy exchange. Man and woman are created in such a way that they balance each other in perfect equilibrium and together form a mighty powerful dynamo of neutralized force. It will depend upon each one individually how this force will be used or whether it reaches the alchemical chamber to become transmuted from fire into light. When woman assumes her real power, man can truly rise to his.

SEXUAL, EMOTIONAL AND COMPETITIVE LOVE VS. INTUITIONAL AND SPIRITUAL LOVE

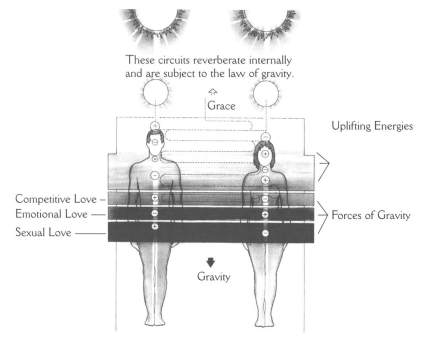

These circuits reverberate internally and are subject to the law of gravity.

Grace

Uplifting Energies

Competitive Love
Emotional Love
Sexual Love

Forces of Gravity

Gravity

In order to help with your own self diagnosis, you could try working on the following questions which are part of the workshop, Karma and Sexuality, at the Centre for Inner Alchemy:

1   What is my concept of femininity? Masculinity? What does it mean for me to be a woman (or man)? How do I see the opposite sex's role?

2   What generates my sexuality? In other words what motivates, me? What 'turns me on'?

3   How does my sexuality express itself? (Include the obvious and the not so obvious ways in everyday activities, including creativity and work.)

4   Which is my power of attraction? That is to say, how do I attract partners?

5   Which are my restrictions or limitations regarding sexuality and the sexual act? Intimacy?

6   How do I experience loss (or gain) in my use of sexual energy?

7   How do I relate to 'surrender'? 'Trust'? 'Power'? 'Potency'?

8   Have I ever been attracted to the same sex? (Review your feelings, judgments and opinions about homosexuality.)

9   How do I experience orgasm? (Allow yourself to think openly and naturally about this.) Have I experienced multiple orgasm?

10   What do I like and/or need most from the opposite sex? From members of the same sex?

11   Is there anything I am 'ashamed' about? (Review the ways in which you have misused sexual energy.)

12   Can I live with myself as a sexual being even if I am unable to express this directly? (Can you find creative satisfaction?)

Friendship

Friendship is a very special happening which in its truest and highest sense always evokes the activity of the heart centre. The dynamic of energetic circulation here is predominantly 'other body' oriented. This other body phenomenon is also present in sexual relationships, but there it feeds into and supports the exchange of vital force through the body fluids.

Members of the same sex will trigger one another's mental and emotional development and, as in the case of Latin cultures, if there is enough hugging and affectionate exchange it can trigger healthy body activity which is basically nourished by heart energy.

Friends will be attracted by one another for similar reasons as are couples. These reasons may be induced by the lower chakras (i.e. need-compulsion-exploitation), or they may be caused by genuine admiration and respect. In the latter case they serve to inspire and uplift the inner mechanism of the individual and foster spiritual development.

Rather than predominant chakra activity, in friendship the exchange is largely between body layers. Surrounding the physical polarity of a male body, as suggested in the previous chapter, is a negative emotional polarity which besides representing a focus of activity as a chakra, is also an entire network of subtle body energy surrounding and interpenetrating the body itself. Surrounding this second receptive expression around a male body will appear another positive mental body polarization. The inverse applies to women.

This phenomenon allows for innumerable combinations and patterns of energy exchange which can be immensely gratifying and incentivating at mental, emotional and spiritual levels. An emotionally polarized individual can benefit greatly by his or her friendship with a mentally polarized individual and vice-versa. A mentally polarized person can grow in leaps and bounds through friendship with a spiritually polarized person, as possible in the true relationship between teacher and student. This explains why many friendships are essentially more rewarding than competitive sexual relationship. Friendship expresses the purity of sharing and is the most exalted expression of love. It is truly a holy allegiance between two souls devoid of the entanglements and obligations of ordinary relating.

All too often sexual starvation or repression is projected onto friendship, feeding yet more subliminal fantasy and illusion, disillusionment and frustration. This is the basic mechanism behind the expectation and demand which contaminate the altruistic nature of true friendship. Needless to say a relationship can be both sexual and friendly, although, if we take a close look, we will notice that it will lean more to one side or the other. In most friendly sexual relationships there is very little deeply sexual activity.

Chapter Seven

THE ORGASMIC PULSE OF LIFE

Mental activity through the atom of consciousness projects electrical, linear charge. Matter or substance emits magnetic, concentric force-fields. When mind is projected onto matter, a nucleus or creation point is conceived. This is a kind of material atom as a focus of manifestation. When two such creation points interact in any relationship the effect produced is a multiplication of electrical irradiation and magnetic oscillations. Relationships repeat the process of creation. The sexual set between members of opposite polarity amplifies this phenomenon considerably as it multiplies life and births, the forms through which life expresses itself. (See illustrations overleaf.)

In the case of the human sexual act, the subconscious intent of the participants determines the quality of the creation which will be energized at the moment of orgasm.

There is massive literature on the subject of the human orgasm. Modern sex behaviour research and ancient Taoist, Hindu and Tibetan Tantric texts are quite popular today. The first sources tend to be technically oriented and are often mechanical and depersonalized. The second sources are more humane but far too complicated and time consuming for the modern mind.

How the individual conceives of his body and how he operates his mind is of paramount importance. The primary issue here is to reformulate our ideas concerning the vitality of sexuality and the experience of orgasm. We seem to have lost the capacity to participate with the sensory activity of the body deeply and wholly. This sensitivity may be regained individually when the internal health and resilience of the body organs, and particularly of the nervous system (whose repair is urgently needed) is achieved and the mind is trained to co-participate with the body.

Orgasm is a natural phenomenon. It is something that happens at all levels of creation, from the atomic particle to the solar complex. It is something which happens within the physical body continuously, with or without our awareness of it. Greater pleasure and optimum use result as a natural consequence of living consciously within matter. The awareness that participates with this creativity far transcends the mechanism of the rational mind.

A child allowed to experience his body spontaneously, although not yet self conscious, lives within a certain awareness of orgasmic activity which manifests as joy, happiness, vitality. Orgasm includes pulsation and flow, the natural ebullience of life in the flesh. Nature acts between individuals regardless of age or sex, playing upon the polarities not only at the level of the physical body but among the layers surrounding it. Mind is meant to co-participate with the body and not to substitute or interfere with its rhythms. Every cell in our bodies is in a state of orgasm naturally.

When an individual whose consciousness is outwardly focused feels sensation he will decode it through any one of a number of ways. Rather than feeling sensation naturally, it will be tinged by the thought process involved. Most often sensation is coloured by sexual overtones. Sex becomes an obsession, an insatiable craving, a secret addiction, a dangerous thrill or a curse before which we apparently have no control. But this need not be so. Sexuality is the natural feeling – sensation of life – it in no way implies a determined expression.

When a centred individual feels sensation he will acknowledge it as an expression of natural creative cyclic law. He might even assume the position of benefactor of this mighty precious life through him. As guardian, he might delight immensely with the pleasure of experiencing life directly. He will know that this activity does not originate from outside himself. His atom of consciousness, poised within the heart chamber, perceives activity from the administrative centre of the permanent atoms without any intermediary agents to qualify the perception. He is self-sufficient, which does not mean that he is any less reverent of life as it expresses around and outside of him. He knows that all life is One. He knows this because he lives this. It is childish to think that one cannot experience the fullness of life within the body without a partner. If and when a partner is needed, nature itself will provide us with one. If we remember that in order to attract that which we wish to attract we need to vibrate at the same frecuency, we might stop obsessing with the belief that without a partner we will not achieve fulfilment, or enlightenment, and start being the best that we can be. In other words stop feeding fear. Once we ourselves are at a place where transmutation can happen, we no longer need the other to produce it. Without neediness nature can take over. What this means is that when all neediness is gone, needs are naturally met, as Arthur Janov, my first trainer, used to say years ago in speaking of emotional needs and the Primal Experience.[7]

THE PROCESS OF CREATION 1A

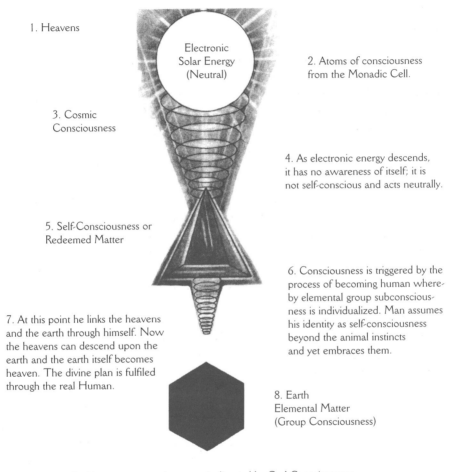

1. Heavens

Electronic
Solar Energy
(Neutral)

2. Atoms of consciousness
from the Monadic Cell.

3. Cosmic
Consciousness

4. As electronic energy descends,
it has no awareness of itself; it is
not self-conscious and acts neutrally.

5. Self-Consciousness or
Redeemed Matter

6. Consciousness is triggered by the
process of becoming human whereby elemental group subconsciousness is individualized. Man assumes
his identity as self-consciousness
beyond the animal instincts
and yet embraces them.

7. At this point he links the heavens
and the earth through himself. Now
the heavens can descend upon the
earth and the earth itself becomes
heaven. The divine plan is fulfiled
through the real Human.

8. Earth
Elemental Matter
(Group Consciousness)

In this way too cosmic energy is directed by God-Consciousness
when Man returns to the Father and becomes one with the source.

The first step is becoming aware of energy within the body and letting it just be there.
We don't need to do anything with it. It simply is. We learn to enjoy its presence
and marvel at its movements, its dance, its circuits within us. Unless we can do this,
even with the perfect partner, orgasm in the fullest sense will not be possible. In

order to participate in the orgasm we must first be a passive and reverent witness within it. It is the very essence of cosmic explosion/implosion within, catalyzing the endless cycles of destruction and creation.

THE PROCESS OF CREATION 1B

The Process of Creation: Creation Points

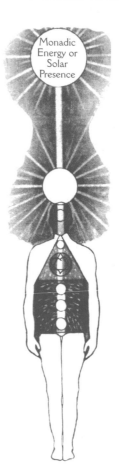

Monadic Energy or Solar Presence

1. Trajectory of the Great Atom of Consciousness (atman) as it forges a line of force upon which the various vehicles for consciousness will be built.

2. The Creation of Cosmic Consciousness. Real power drawn through refined and sustained use of faculties from accumulated light momentum.

3. Personal will attuned to higher will as the divine plan or Natural Order.

4. The Creation of the Causal Body. Accumulation of redeemed matter/substance within the consciusness of the trans-personal flexible personality as Self consciousness.

5. Elemental matter refined and directed by the focus of consciousness.

6. The Creation of the Personality as Group Planetary Subconsciousness.

7. Elemental matter acting through concentric, magnetic force, grouped into standard group form.

Earth Substance/Matter

If we are fearful of intensity, be that of the senses or the emotions, rather than a blessing orgasm is perceived as sheer torture which one must brace against at all costs. Only a flexible-personality structure which has already begun to relate to life as movement and pure experience of energy phenomena can remain poised, centred and participatory. When orgasm happens there is no centre, there is no form, there is no referential. It is pure concentricity, 'Am-ness' within the Chaos.

THE PROCESS OF CREATION 2

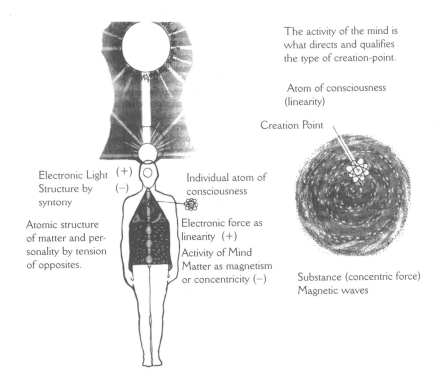

The activity of the mind is what directs and qualifies the type of creation-point.

Atom of consciousness (linearity)

Creation Point

Electronic Light (+) Structure by (−) syntony

Individual atom of consciousness

Atomic structure of matter and personality by tension of opposites.

Electronic force as linearity (+)
Activity of Mind Matter as magnetism or concentricity (−)

Substance (concentric force) Magnetic waves

The creation of karma occurs when opposite polarities (+, −) meet and form a creation point, (crystallization). The same mind (activity of light) qualifies or directs the creation into trans-personal modalities. At this point the polarity of the heart nexus has changed (to −) and another creation point is built upon contact with electronic substance (+), now operating under the law of syntony.

Orgasmic activity at cellular and energetic levels is the participation of such creations at different levels of life.

Male vs Female Orgasm

The different orgasms which men and women experience relate to their obvious polarization within matter. Men's physical orgasm follows a linear modality, accelerating rapidly and directly to the goal. Upon reaching a ceiling it must overflow and release itself, unless the man is trained to withhold ejaculation and redirect that build-up through his body. Many men are unable to withstand the high voltages which woman on the other hand conducts.

Women's orgasm follows a slower, steadier orbit with step-like scales of progressive intensification which, because of her inward anatomy can sustain increasingly high levels of frequency. In this sense woman is orgasmically superior to man. At the point where most men reach orgasm a woman is barely beginning to accelerate. What is considered ordinary peak orgasm in men is only a third of the potential that women possess.

Ideally the male would learn to control his orgasm while accompanying the female in reaching her potential. This will release more and higher energy through him. For this to happen a certain degree of technique is required, a technique which accompanies but does not replace the psychological state of the partners and the level of mutual respect which both must have achieved.

Both men and women could de-emphasize peak orgasm and learn to prolong the sexual experience into subtler, finer modalities when both parties have experience in sustaining higher levels of frequencies within themselves. Instead of succumbing (usually by incapacity to resist) to release and overflow, the training required is to contain the energies while continuing to circulate them. The dense energy currents are directed into creating circuits between the partners. From this already high peak a new higher climb is initiated. An analogy may be drawn to one's own relationship to the world. Sustaining intensity and rechanneling refined frequencies is the science of all relationship.

Women find practices which require containment easier to perform. Males are confronted yet again with a subtle mind trap. Whereas control is directed by the mind, the practice of ejaculation control and semen retention without physical consciousness can be extremely dangerous. The art is to be able to do this cooperating with the body. Energy can circulate through the Microcosmic Orbit (see a later description of this practice for both men and women) and return to the blood, whereby it accellerates the function of oxygen (light) that will furnish higher states of consciousness.

The normal, natural and ideal state for relating sexually is a relaxed, aware, cocreational activity. The best lovers are they who know themselves internally and can participate consciously with the movement of energy, flowing over the peaks and valleys, gently but steadily harnessing the peaks, and softly, firmly raising the valleys. This is the Tao, the endless movement which through activity and repose is life.

The usual ways of gratification for homosexuals involve either anal or oral sex, neither of which really furnishes healthy equilibrium in the internal organs or in the energetic bodies. In male homosexuals, a hyper-activation of the emotional body, the next layer to which the energies move in an attempt to circulate, provokes obsessive and compulsive emotionality. A super-activation of the positive pole at the base chakra violates the tactile circuitry, aggravating an already intense need in the male homosexual for excessive cutaneous touch and sensuality. Added to this, the deposit of vital force at the base of the spine which is stimulated during anal sex, becomes depleted, debilitating the male homosexual of his vital essence, a chief cause for the breakdown of the immune system.

Oral sex, although widely practised presents a danger when used as a replacement for sexual intercourse. Practitioners of oral sex, be they lesbian, gay or heterosexual, risk depleting the delicate frequencies of the throat centre which enable higher etheric contact. Since energy always travels from the highest to the lowest, the more intense frequencies of the higher centre often over-stimulate the lower centres.

The product of two negative polarities meeting at the physical level results in a positive (male) charge which seeks expression at the physical and emotional levels of women. Many lesbians are compulsively aggressive. Their behaviour is marked by displays of competitiveness, anger, suspicion, isolation and a general coarseness which has nothing to do with cultural refinement or education.

From the technical point of view, Taoists suggest that homosexuals practice meditations which charge them with the opposite polarity. In the case of women this would indicate a conscious absorption of the energy of fire from the sun. For males the charging is to be sought from the surface of the earth itself. Both men and women are asked to open up their deeper body circuits so that they can filter the healing properties of the opposite polarity which their partners do not possess, into and through their bodies.

The motivation for homosexuality must be sought in the psychology of the individual. I have met many homosexuals, particularly in the days when my practice was in New York City, who had sought refuge in homosexuality out of habit and convenience. In some cases tremendous fear arises out of the possible intimacy with a person of the opposite polarity (which of course catalyzes terrific forces). It is important that the homosexual examine his thoughts, desires and motivations if he wishes to free himself, as anybody else, from the burdens of karma. All too often he or she feels alienated and as a reaction-formation becomes all too proud about his preference.

It is not only possible but deeply nourishing to tune into one's partner of the opposite sex in order to participate of the subtle energy flow between polarities. This has been a method of self-healing for millenia in the East which Mahatma Gandhi himself used in order to restore balance and vitality. Knights of the Templar Order, who were committed to celibacy, also practised nonsexual merging with another. This level of interchange can be practised at any stage of development.

One does **not** need a partner in order to circulate sexual energy. It is in fact easier to establish this ideal circulation without the distracting excitement and heat of another person. Once sex energy has been identified through awareness, an individual can balance the male and female poles which exist inside the body proper.

The most sublime flow is achieved by the individual who has already mastered outer sexual drive and has attained a certain level of spiritual self-knowledge. Here the energy does not move outward to the senses but inward to the root of the centres, seeking the man or woman within. 'Man or woman within' means reaching to that higher union between the lower sexual pole at the base chakra and the heart centre, through the inner passages of the centres.

Only when the person is rooted in the modality of the heart can he absorb energy directly from the universal, all-pervading life force all around. It is not recommended that this be attempted without personal body knowledge first, the conscious maintenance of a healthy full-body energy circulation, and the stabilization of a flexible-personality character structure. There is every possibility of higher energies aggravating lower personality traits or creating greater illusion, when awareness is not sustained at the level of true self-consciousness. It is precisely to counteract widespread misuse of higher energies channelled into personalistic modalities that this book has been written.

Energy Exchange and the Creation of the Flame

Drawing from ancient sources, Torkom Saradayan has published illuminating information on the esoteric undertone of sexual energy exchange. Man injects force through secretions into the woman at the moment of orgasm. Woman qualifies and reproduces this force through higher emotion and returns it to man as joy and vitality. If she is not an evolved woman, this force is emotionally polluted by personalistic traits. When returned to the man through the heart centre, the possibility of transmutation for both opens up new dimensions.

Orgasm both attracts and expresses creative forces. It has been observed that during orgasm the vital aura of both partners and the etheric centres of woman (even without ovulation) fuse to form an electromagnetic nucleus for the reception of the silver cord from a monadic cell. The orgasmic impulse generates such intense energy that stability at the level of the lower bodies is needed to act as grounding, before the individuals can harness and sustain such creative forces. If both partners are properly prepared and present, this energy can transport their consciousness into higher states with full awareness.

The impact of both atoms of consciousnes as they attune into one at the heart is tremendous. Perception occurs through the upper centres opening possibilities that a common orgasm descending into the lower range of vibrations cannot. Two ordinary individuals, even if they should happen to reach orgasms simultaneously, are in separate worlds of fantasy, manipulation and desire.

Orgasm is only the beginning of transcendental union. We seem to have lost the possibility, and with that the knowledge evoked as two individuals journey through higher perception together. If the couple is able to remain together and in physical merger, the entire trajectory of consciousness opens up.

The tendency in common relations is to separate immediately after orgasm, have a snack, smoke a cigarette, or fall asleep – anything so as not to be faced with the awareness of oneself and, what's more frightening, with the depth of life, or the emptiness produced by their lack of participation within it.

In orgasm individuals are invited to surrender to life, not to one another. When orgasm is allowed to happen in tense-free relaxed conditions of silence, the inner excitation recalls the very rhythms of creation. In such encounters a tiny flame is produced. This flame heals and nourishes the nervous system, purifies the discord within the emotional body, and opens up blocked passages and electrical circuits. It consumes all negative elements present in both partners and in their surroundings, actually clearing a room of unwanted thoughtforms.

This flame is not the same as the electromagnetic nucleus. The nucleus is formed by subtle matter and relates to physical atomic patterns. The flame is a product of light and can only be created by syntony when there already is consciousness within each person. This flame is created by the merger of positive and negative electricity within both partners and constitutes the basic ingredient for transmutation. The increased proportion of light in matter catalyses the emergence of a new quality of matter out of the old. This phenomenon constitutes the blending of hearts called the alchemical marriage.

The ideal marriage does not emphasize sexual union but rather an essential unity, a mutual honouring, and represents the attunement of two consciousnesses, two higher selves. It implies a union at the physical level, a blending of the emotional bodies, a syncronization at the level of the mind, and an overlapping of the two souls. Marriage unites the lower self with the higher self through the medium of a partner. The help offered by the presence of the other is indirect, not a meddling intervention into the psyche of the other. Having a partner means greater responsability not lesser. People should understand this and better prepare themselves for the added influx of forces, energies, behavioural patterns and circumstancial burdens which a relationship naturally places upon an individual.

The onslaught of blame, accusation and humiliation which often results from misplaced expectations stamps the death of the relationship even before the possibility for consciousness arises. Only when we love ourself do we have something beautiful and worthwhile to offer another. The other is meant to be an inspiration, a symbol and not a substitute for contact with the Innermost Self. When the energy which has been generated by a couple together has no other expression than one another, there is every chance that it will breed stalemate and discord.

The Other Is Only A Doorway To The Self. Be grateful, in reverent respect... but honour the Self.

Suggestions for Sexual Relating

Discipline is an inner posture predicated on impeccability and a knowledge of the rhythms of life. When a person knows himself in like manner, he or she naturally sets economical uses of precious energies and timing. The suggestions given here follow common sense and were taken by Torkom Saradayan from remotest antiquity. I have modified some and added more. Each individual is meant to apply his or her own rules based upon his natural rhythm.

Sex for the ancient sages was regarded as a sacramental meeting, a meditation, an encounter with the infinite. It was not a need predicated on urgency. The cyclic activity of nature was studied.

Sexual rhythm cannot be dictated by imposition. It arises from mutual conscious accord. Cyclical sexual contact is best decided in advance. Most sources will agree that intercourse should be avoided in extreme states, under intoxicating drugs, during intense weather conditions, when tired or bored, and after big meals.

It was observed that man's greatest sexual power occurs in the springtime. This means that at other times of the year we should not expect the same inspiration.

Showering should precede and not follow the sexual act in order to allow enough time for the subtle body energies to become absorbed into the body complex.

It is best to not have sexual intercourse during menstruation. During this time a woman is strongly subject to astral and decay-producing lunar influences. She can affect the male adversely, catalyzing the negative side of his passions. The ancients always recommended that woman sleep separately during these times and that she consciously direct herself into positive modalities of expression.

The romanticism surrounding the idea of the full moon is largely emotional indulgence. Sexual relations are best avoided two days before the full moon and up to two days after, again for the impact which the powerfully charged astral atmosphere has over mankind. Police statistics in Sao Paulo (Brazil) indicate that the major incidence of sexual crimes occurs during the full moon.

Oral sex is best de-emphasized. Recent studies suggest that the emphasis placed upon oral sex may be due to the fact that many men have lost their sensitivity at the level of their sexual organ. Instead pleasure is registered through extreme and excessively mental means. On the other hand women have lost the ability to feel internally, preferring to remain at the level of clitoral sensation without learning how to transfer and deepen the initial stimulation into the deepest recesses of the vaginal walls.

Pornography and stimulants are sought to satisfy man's outwardly-focussed mental preoccupation. All schools of spiritual knowledge prohibit their use which, for obvious reasons, augments the quantity and quality of elemental thoughtforms that interfere with fine sensitivity and genuine mutual appreciation.

Masturbation is common in the initial stages of sexual training to gain awareness of the energetic patterns produced. It was never meant to be used as a substitute for the sexual act, as a tension reliever, or as an antidote for boredom.

Sexual energy is a fuel which serves to transform, transmute and transfigure. It must be used wisely, creating periods of total abstinence in order to regenerate and preserve the sacredness of the substance produced and the sublime function which is serves.

Marriage offers a natural protection. When one of the partners has sexual relations with someone other than his partner, he breaks the subtle energy links with the former partner. If the partner is sensitive he or she may even detect when and with whom this happens. These links are created horizontally at the level of the chakras in order to conduct forces and circulate energies. When these links are severed through extra-marital relations they cannot always be reconstructed. The broken links then drain forces or energies, which hook up with sinister forces at the astral plane, overstimulating the lower centres and attacking the upper ones. Promiscuity or sexual libertinage has never been approved by esoteric schools, for the simple reason that a breach of loyalty breaks the links. Horizontal magnetic links between couples can carry over after the death of one of the partners as well, creating anguish and confusion to the partner who is alive and seeks a new companion.

Workshop participants often bring up the subject of poligamy in ancient tribal systems. Within those cultures, where a man is legally married to several wives, or a woman to several husbands, it is the natural law of the place or time. Ideally there is harmonious and respectful consent, if not deep attunement among the people involved, creating a spiritual unit. The unit is the means for spiritual awakening and not the individual relationships within that unit.

In our Western culture open marriages often occur where one or both partners agree to enter into extra-marital relations. At this point sexuality within the marriage ceases to be a vehicle for energetic transformation and the relationship becomes friendship, however beautiful or convenient that might be. The chemistry which produces the elixir for sexual transmutation is constructed upon concentrated forces which can only be produced within an individual, committed conscious unit. In some rare cases this happens outside marriage with another person when the relationship with the legal partner is not a sexual one. We are not living in ancient times and must take stock of the essence behind many ancient practices to find the appropriate application to our times.

Ritualistic Merging

The rituals suggested in the following segment are meant to serve as inspiration to couples who want to re-establish the mystery of the sacrosant relationship between the sexes.

After setting the day and preparing in advance the time and location, the atmosphere, music, and whatever else you like, meet when you are both rested and alert. Let your surroundings reflect the purity of your intentions.

You should both prepare yourselves by spending time alone, in communion with yourself. In this way you create the right tension, or polarity, for meeting the other. Your frame of mind should be one of expectancy. You will meet with your counterpart: one god meeting with his goddess, the heavens meeting with the earth, water meeting with fire.

Don't confuse expectancy with expectation or stress. Expectancy describes a patient, ardent waiting... like waiting for the magnificence of daybreak after a long night of vigil. And have no artificial props for stimulation. Try to have as few items as possible if you have decided to ritually feed one another in the tantric fashion. This means small bowls of rice or fruit, a symbolic token rather than a pig-out; small cups of wine, not a whole bottle. You want to remain aware and present with maximum energy and vitality.

Let the music be sensuous without being coarse. Let there be lighting enough to see the other's face and stand revealed without shame in humbled glory, vulnerable and yet strong, an individual and yet aware of the other as part of yourself. Speak very little if at all.

You are now ready to sit before one another in meditative contemplation. In Hindu Tantra, which is considerably more devotional than other esoteric sexual schools, the partners would meet in this way, without physical contact, for a full year before they were allowed to touch. (This would be impossible in our times!) In all traditions emotions are refined. The other is never seen as an object. He or she is a messenger from God, the other half of yourself.

Facing one another now, feel the presence of the other with your entire body. You may hum or chant together to intensify, through resonance, the vibratory activity of your organism which must be highly sensitized to detect the nuances of move-ment and circulation of energies within and through you, and now to feel the impact of the opposite polarity stimulating, exciting, calling you.

Do this still without touching, and if the visual stimulation is too distracting for you to feel yourself feeling the other, then close your eyes until you reconnect with your-self. This stage can go on for ten minutes or longer.

Now you may join hands or delicately touch fingertips to awaken the subtle cur-rents of electricity at etheric levels. It is especially powerful to coordinate your ener-gies through breathing. Experiment with different combinations. One may inhale while the partner exhales, creating a fine flow of force between the heart and third eye. The woman exhales, visualising a flow from her heart into her man, as he absorbs in his heart and exhales, sending a flow from his third eye into her. You may want to try this with your eyes closed in order to build up for the impact of the visual meeting in the next stage. Allow the energies to pool and build to a peak before you pass onto the next stage.

Gaze into your partner's left eye and allow the projections or facial distortions that appear to drift by, remaining poised in your heart centre. Some prefer to gaze at the spot between the eyes at the bridge of the nose. The eyes remain softly receptive, never aggressively staring, demanding or intruding.

Here you may want to close your eyes once again, now to feel yourself softly merging with your lover's energy field, always acknowledging one another within the Alchemical Alignment. Remain in this light merger for a while. In some instances the bodies are contained within a cape or sheet to also seal the bio-physical energies within the partners' auric field.

Treat kissing as the sacramental prelude that it is, knowing that saliva too is a vital fluid which contains and conducts life force. Be especially aware of the electrical currents that are created as you kiss your partner on the mouth or over the body. Let yourselves bless one another's body parts, not as fetishism but as appreciation. In order to distribute energies and sensations deeply into the tissue, you may want to massage one another's full body (if you have not done so already), before you join physically.

Once united, remain joined for a while in relaxed expectancy, circulating the energies and from time to time moving enough to generate greater momentum, but not to reach orgasm. Keep the breath deep and full throughout. Pause to absorb, circulate and integrate. Alternate between movement and stillness. Prolong the moment of orgasm as much as possible. Stay aware and sensitive to your own sensing feeling-perceptive experience and, throughout, gratefully acknowledge the presence of the other and the miracle of life's flow through you. Take time to create your own dance of energies.

Please understand that the power that you absorb from your own body is the power that stays with you. The vitalizing effect of the other's energy within you only serves to trigger and awaken your own; if not used intelligently, it will wear out eventually, leaving you depleted. Initiation into the inner mysteries of nature is given by woman, but it cannot be bestowed without an infusion of male energy as a catalyst.

Couples will experience new openings during love-making, quantum leaps in feeling and awareness. The battle of the sexes reproduces the impulse of life. One is not to enter into this battle with the purpose of competing and conquering but rather in the spirit of gamesmanship which matches grace and skill. This skill must be cultivated by each person individually. Train yourself to collect your energies in the heart and in the region of the 'hara' – the natural warehouses for power.

Love is a mystery which cannot be taught. It can only be experienced by the courageous. You can live happily in love only if you are in harmony with the principles of life. There is no greater love than life. Once the sex force has been conserved and transformed, meditation serves to balance the male and female poles which exist inside everyone, culminating in spontaneous inner orgasm. This orgasm as the fullness of life is the natural result of consciousness and the birthright of every human being.

Chapter Eight

THE WAY OF LOVE AND LIFE

We embody in an individual way the very same materials as any other human. The essential molecular pattern is identical in all, as is the capacity and need for emotional involvement and mental stimulation. This means that the three lower bodies are constructed of the same substance and mould. Some of our animal brothers also share this physical pattern.

What is it then that sets us apart from other expressions of life? Our capacity to know and to love as a creative process of irradiation. The way of the heart. Jesus, the greatest spokesman for the language of the heart embodied and exemplified this way: loving God above all things and loving one another as ourselves, in humility, respect and cooperation.

But what is this 'love'? Surely it can't be the emotional treacle which passes for it, the blind devotion, the projected fear and insatiability, the yearning for someone 'up there' who will come to save us because we are feeble-minded, fearful and passive!

Energetically love is a substance which is emitted from the heart centre. As the flame in the heart ignites truly and fire becomes light, it joins up with the primal vortex of intelligent activity and life-directing processes in the centre of the head to become wisdom. This means that intelligence enlightened by sentient awareness of the whole is the key – the one and only – to the evolution of consciousness. This happens naturally, through a life lived fully in the body and on the Earth.

The first part of the spiritualization process happens within the lower chamber of the heart during the consumption of karma (the transcendence of the attachment to both 'good' and 'bad' karma). This burning process corresponds to the stages during which the individual honours life within himself by incorporating bodily flexibility, emotional stability and greater understanding. Egoism dissolves and the heart begins to open. It is a long and difficult process of living what we learned and reorienting our activities and relationships in the world.

During this period the individual falls into the collective unconsciousness of the lower chakras many times. As we slowly acquire dominion over these impulses, we summon up power which goes into building character, that causal body which will direct our energies in the following stages. This nexus resonates in the area of the heart centre.

The second stage of growth consists of maintaining stability within the newly organized behaviour pattern. At this point we begin to use our faculty of expanding light within the heart chamber, which connotes transforming everything we touch into gold. In this way we begin to emit a frequency which evokes a new kind of substance. This substance has been called 'bodhicitta' by Buddhists and could be translated as the irradiation of goodwill. The true function of the heart, that of an alchemical chamber, expands from that of transmuting the substance of the personal world and body, into transforming or affecting the substance of the world-at-large.

This is the real function of love. Far from being an emotion used for personal gratification, it is a state of Mind in the amplest sense of the word, where it includes all of man's faculties now subdued by the intelligent, directing principle which Mind in essence is. Now the 'kingdom of heaven' is not only man's own interiority, grounded in a healthy functioning at the level of the lower chakras (focussed at the navel) it is also everywhere man is, because he Is. Love has been the process, the state of consciousness, and the irradiation of the entire organism.

Whereas we need to use a communication system common to all of humanity, in a state of love words acquire a different vibration and convey a more complex wholistic vision. The language of the heart is silence without the presence of past-future thinking. True silence dictates the ability to be present and fully, consciously aware and responsive to life's processes – aesthetically, poetically. Poetry, like the figure of the Christ Self, like the images of angels... inspires, uplifts and momentarily transposes one into a world of silence and beauty. This activates a vibrational frequency within the individual which is akin to that of his own heart. For a moment at least, he partakes of a subtle alchemy.

Poetry, however, draws from the conscious and unconscious reservoir of human emotionality with its obvious pros and cons. Were we to rescue the dynamics of emotionality from its impulsive permutations we would discover that emotions contain emissions (the movement of energies) which are triggered off by the intricate webbing of the nervous system, which serves to amplify energy.

Whereas the training has consisted in learning to control the unconscious activity of this nervous system which creates the incessant projections of feelings, the ability for expanding and generating energy remains intact. We learn to control and pool emotional energy in order to harness it and direct it into other 'higher' ways. The emotional body becomes the servant-vehicle.

We must retain our ability for aware emotional response. This ability is lost by many sincere seekers who, in many cases jaded by common emotionality have been severely wounded in their own relationships. Many escape into asceticism and retreatism because they are unable to give and withstand ordinary affection. We cannot excuse insensitivity or isolation. Part of giving is learning to receive whatever the other person can give. This is the art of relationship.

Natural, human, personal love is essential for growth. Love in the sense of a fraternal spirit is often absent, depriving the individual of a genuine feeling of being appreciated. Love involves walking together through the small steps of daily existence and lending a hand. In order for it to work effectively it must be bestowed. Emotions are the lessons in love. 'Never be ashamed of crying', I tell my trainees. No one is perfect. And because we aren't we can help one another as nature naturally calls.

It is the heart which serves as the organ for perception and activity in the higher life; its mechanism must work optimally. Like the chords of a fine string instrument, our resonance ability must be both tight and flexible to run the gamut of rainbow tones which sing life's melodies. Transmutation is both a science and an art, which cannot happen without love.

The Quest for Union

Relationship at the human organic level responds to the attraction which exists between the lower and the higher selves. The union which we seek outside with another is symbolic of the unity we seek with our own monadic cell. Completion and fulfilment can only occur at the highest levels of our being.

Except under very special and rare circumstances, where the individual's biological, psychological and causal modality is already evolved, man cannot attain to this sublime unity with the Self alone. He needs a relationship with the opposite polarity, the opposite electromagnetic field, which will prepare him for that unio mystica which the ultimate alchemical marriage with the Self offers. From this inherent need arise the friendships and passions, the psychological interactions at all levels which pave the way and bring one closer to oneself and God. The egoism of the personality offers a great resistance in an effort to preserve its identity – an identity which is destructured only to re-emerge purified and transformed upon contact with the source.

Sex essentially expresses duality: matter and spirit, feminine and masculine, negative and positive, mother and father. The primordial sexual attraction strives to fuse man and woman, man and his soul, man and God, and ultimately Man and the Universe. Each merger marks the birth of an offspring, beginning with the child of the specie, the birth or creation of consciousness (which is the causal self), the 'anthropus', and finally Universal Man.

Through our intellect we generate both the force which drives us towards as well as against the ultimate merger with the opposite pole, creating artificial excitation and tension. Unless there is excitation, ordinary humanity does not seem to feel attraction. It is as if we have lost touch with natural appeal and the incentive for meeting with challenge. Common sexual attraction has its roots in the fear of aloneness that confrontation with the magnitude and majesty of the universe within evokes in the existing personality.

Character and Consciousness

Character is the result of a flexible personality which serves itself of energetic complexes known as archetypes. Archetypes plug into monadic energies and by connecting with them we may serve ourself of qualities which we may use appropriately. In order for us to be able to do this we must know ourself and possess a firm ability to direct our lower instincts. Through the fluidity and adaptability of a flexible personality we can avail ourself of archetypes which may not be directly related to our own more usual style. We can become a conscious actor on the stage of life. Acting here does not refer to being phoney in any way but to lending consciousness to an individual pattern of behaviour that contains an energetic complex of force.

Classic archetypes include the pantheon of gods and goddesses of both Eastern and Western tradition. They convey forces that exist within each monadic unit as individualities, figures which codify and access energies for personal and transcendent use.

Archetypes are successfully and intentionally accessed by consciousness when the flexible personality creates a solid base for expression in the world. This solid base is known as character. Character should be built strongly but flexibly enough that it can withstand many kinds and varieties of voltages. An archetype is a kind of energy accumulator which feeds and animates the character of the seeker built upon a flexible personality.

As God expresses Himself through the male specie, the following individual characteristics are expressed in the unique manner in which his trans-individuality can express: leadership, sincerity, intellectual keenness, nobility, creativity, magnanimity, a sense of real justice, integrity and impeccability. Each of these inherently masculine qualities denote an inner consciousness at work which perceives the world multidimensionally and concentrically. These qualities represents an inner assessment and intentionality having nothing to do with what appears as outer manifestation.

As God expresses Herself through the female specie, she will come to express as only she can, the unique attributes of her gender: kindness and forgiveness, patience, generosity, wisdom, emotional control, economy and practicality, simplicity and joy of life. This does not mean that she has to act like a passive little flower. Above all woman is Mother. This maternity is psychological and spiritual, an emanation of her nature which is neither symbolic nor emotional. It is an irradiation which heals, stimulates, inspires and illumines the world. Women need to understand this deeply. In this understanding they can heal themselves and arise majestically to embrace man, helping him to become himself and to guide our world.

Man's Individual Path into Consciousness

Whether he is in a relationship or whether he is alone, whether he is Black or Caucasian, Indian or Oriental, whether his path is one of devotion or of knowledge, of science or in the active service of humanity, the member of the male specie will follow a particular path in the development and consequent building of consciousness.

The natural evolutionary pathway for men begins with his own capacity to be in his body in a healthy, stable, moderate and practical modality. From here he connects to his discriminating, non-judgmental analytical faculties at his second positive pole at the level of the solar-plexus, facing the biggest challenge anyone can face, the confrontation with the tendency of the mind to impart false certainty.

If man succeeds in disidentifying himself from the labelling process of the concrete mind, he moves to the positive modalities at the throat centre or the buddhic level, enabling him to access universal mind and knowledge which sets him free from the lower forces. At this point, monadic impulse becomes available. His way is paved.

Since it is an extremely tricky affair to offset the powerful illusions created by the concrete mind, few men make it into buddhic levels on their own. When they do, they often lack the emotional power that is so important for the needs of spirituality today. Without this emotional flexibility he appears harsh and brittle, distant and authoritarian.

In order to attain to the state of androgyny which merger with his own heart provides, the mother figure in his life plays a paramount role. For some men this input has first been given to him by his carnal mother. For many this imput comes through the woman in his life. Without this foundation at the emotions, the leap from consciousness at the level of the solar plexus to the third eye is virtually impossible. With the influence of a woman to activate cellular transmutation and trigger the emotional juiciness of the second chakra, in order to catalyze the heart centre, man finds a transitionary equilibrium at the level of the throat centre. From there he can begin the stabilization procedure at the third eye.

Even though it is a long and twisted tale for both man and woman, the trajectory of relationships with the opposite sex is still the most direct route to true transcendence, taking men into the visionariness of his own atmic centre through the pathway of the heart. Man's path is perhaps the most difficult, but it is also the most glorious, when the son becomes one with the Father at the Source.

INDIVIDUAL PATHWAYS INTO CONSCIOUSNESS

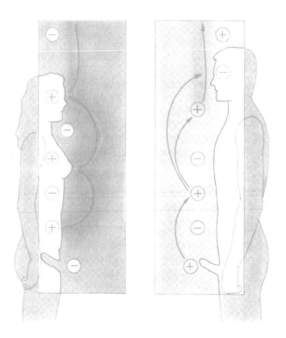

Woman's Individual Path into Consciousness

We already know that woman's strength is also her weakness: her emotional nature. If she is able to define herself adequately through a feeling knowledge of herself as an individual and in the world, she can easily avail herself of the tremendous potential inherent in the heart centre, which accesses the full activation of her positively polarized third eye or atmic body of consciousness and from there, enlightenment. It is much easier for woman to attain to this alone, than it is for man.

Woman faces the greatest difficulty when she is unable to gain her personal identity, something which is hard to come by in today's male-dominated culture. Only through her emotions can she attain individualization, including the dominion and control over her own body and the enjoyment and satisfaction of being in matter. This part of the learning process can be facilitated by relationship with the right male who will honour and reveal her to herself. But this relationship, either within the context of a couple or in the world-at-large brings the added dangers and confusions of the mental complex.

Hers is the path from the emotions to the intuition of the heart, which is where her mental activities actually flourish, bypassing the dangers of the concrete mind to find the Great Mother who was always within.

Aloneness

Despite the freedom granted by some of the more enlightened relationships, there comes a time when each individual needs to be alone (and this usually occurs at different times, which makes the whole thing more difficult). If there is an emotional undertone of addiction in the relationship, this can cause serious problems. In the case of couples, if they already have an established pattern of separate space the problem is diminished somewhat.

Strangely, aloneness is dictated by the opening of the heart centre. When this begins to happen, the individual finds that he cannot relate emotionally in the same ways that he related to his partner, his children, his parents and friends. He appears unloving to others and even to himself, until the new modalities of the heart are acknowledged and integrated. This is a problem that many of my students face.

As the person with genuine compassion tries to accommodate to the demands or real needs of his environment, he enters into great conflicts with his sense of growing integrity and authenticity. It is best that this phenomenon be recognized and accepted. It is best that he, or she be allowed to be whatever and whomever he might appear to be. The loss of meaning for the individual as he passes through the white fire of the heart is agonizing. Mystics have referred to it as 'the dark night of the soul', dark enough without the added burdens of emotional expectation from his friends.

During this crisis presented by the opening of the heart, incomprehensible to the emotional nature of ordinary humanity, there may be great periods of crying for no reason at all. It is best that the student of light prepare himself for this by beginning to respect deeply his own process and that of others.

During this stage too the previous egoism often strives to return, sneaking in through the back door so to speak. The individual should position himself in such a way that he is a witness, a poised light within the oceanic matrix that begins to unfold.

We need to understand what the process of consciousness entails. Whereas a certain degree of disillusionment is inevitable, this disillusionment is merely the realization of our unconsciousness and the robotic existence that we have been leading. It serves the purpose of awakening us to the quest, redirecting the impulse for survival into the drive towards perfection. The journey towards consciousness is not for the escapist, the intellectual, or the obsessive. It is a long and arduous journey.

At first one is enamoured with the idea of light. The original period is marked with the same dynamic of projection that one was living under, except that now the projections are 'nobler' and serve to inspire. They are a temporary measure which any teacher who is truly conscious may use to raise the level of aspiration of the individual seeker and strengthen his determination to reach higher.

The Sufis[8] have perfected this method by consciously projecting an Ideal before them and then courting this Ideal. Initiations consist of communicating with this Ideal within and ultimately merging with it, becoming it, and then transcending it, facing and dissolving as a personality in the last stages of enlightenment. Theirs is an artful process of thought-projection and auto-suggestion which is dangerous when attempted by the common person who is only too eagerly looking for something to escape into. A real mystic is very grounded in the earth, in his body, with nature. He develops his mind in order to discern and play with it; in order to co-create with divinity within.

This inherent divinity for the Sufi (what we have come to call the light seed) is worked upon at the level of the heart. Once the heart opens, the rest follows suit. The heart is the mirror upon which all of our feelings, actions, in fact everything, is reflected. The seeker deliberately negates all which is not of the light, choosing with great determination to affirm the positive. He will know reality directly through systematically dissolving his egoism while simultaneously upholding the Ideal.

The heart chamber is the centre of the universe for man as it is for the fetus who grows around the heart, the organic centre of human life. For the Sufi as for the Buddhist, and the Christian, activating the light consciously within the heart is the means whereby enough voltage and momentum is generated to face and conquer the instincts of the lower self. And whereas self-discipline is the trademark of any sincere aspirant, the severity of this determination for the Sufi is tempered with dance, play and celebration, as well as the cultivation of intense positive emotions which will generate enough energy to consume impurities in the self. This lower self is seen to reside within the solar plexus, a centre which is at the receiving end of willed heart-energies. As a constant discipline the Sufi mystic circulates his energies up to the third eye from where he projects it to the solar plexus in the form of a beam of light meant to dissolve personalistic crystallizations.

The Sufi path is aggressive and extroverted, elaborately dramatic but internally simple. The Buddhist path is introverted and somewhat ascetic. The Christian path is emotionally vulnerable and direct. Whatever the path taken by the individual, there is only One Truth. In the Chamber of the heart are many mansions... and there aloneness becomes All-Oneness.

The Power of Forgiveness

We normally think of forgiveness as something passive, rather bland and somewhat boring. In reality forgiveness requires considerable energy and releases incredibly high voltages of electronic force into the system, energies which had been trapped into thoughtforms or isolated into separate compartments of the body. The power behind the force of forgiveness is the power of the monad channelled through the causal nexus.

During the time when we are building the causal self (or growing in self-consciousness), the deposit of light at the centre of the heart grows, attracting to itself the soul-substance resulting from transmuted elemental forms. This 'jewel' or 'sun' acquires a life of its own. As it expands it develops a voice, a touch, a breath. We grow in intimacy with it as the Christ Self.

Esoteric tradition under different approaches supports communication with this life within, calling it the 'soul', 'conscience', or the 'angel', to name only a few. This is also the Ideal of Sufi mysticism. It serves to absorb and transform electronic voltages for our use. In some cases it is seen as a solar angel who serves the function of our own higher self until we are able to grow in amplitude enough to be able to become our own.

The figure of our higher self becomes very real. It is this figure which will act as the bridge between the self and the Self. Until we are able to withstand the impact of Absolute Truth, we serve ourselves of the delightful proximity, with the sweet comfort and inspiration of the light being within. It may sound odd, but aloneness is achieved in stages of artful self-trickery.

An important step towards acknowledgement of the Christ Self within comes through the act of self-forgiveness. Here we actually communicate with the Self and feel it answering us through irradiation. This step marks a definitive entry of the atom of consciousness within the chamber of the heart and serves to remould our behaviour from the horizontal to the vertical modality. It affects our body chemistry, our emotional relating and our mental outlook. Tears are often the outer manifestation of tremendous softening occuring within.

Self-forgiveness is predicated upon a profound and experiential knowledge of the Law. This Law is the unicity of life and truth: the Law of the One, Love. All the articles of the Law recognize that in essence life (that includes us) is One. We begin by recognizing this truth intellectually. We can understand that if God is within, then we are one with that. Somewhat cautiously at first we can affirm that 'I am God'. This can create a conflict when one is also working on the dissolution of egoism. Let us draw an analogy of the heart as an inner child – this child who will 'inherit the kingdom of God'. This child-quality is innocence and purity, but it becomes confused with the demanding, indulgent, stubborn and somewhat spoiled brat who usurps the power of the heart through a monopoly of the emotions. We need to make a clear distinction between innocence and vulnerability, and indulgence and manipulation. Each 'child' will grow in strength and dominance unless we discriminate between them. The first child needs to be allowed to be. The second needs our firm but loving care, affection such as we would give our own children who need to learn self-discipline without violence. It is difficult during the early period to give love and attention to our physical and emotional selves when we are most of the time enraged with the spoiled brat within. We tread the fine line between anger, guilt, and true illumined guidance.

It is especially important to apply the principle of love during the time of anger and fear, or during the self-punishment and denial that we inflict upon ourselves under the guise of working on ourselves. From this arises true understanding and forgiveness. As a Christ Self, we can do this best by accepting that we are indeed loved, always.

When a child is born he brings with him all the genetic programming of the parents which predispose the mental and emotional structure. The basic psychological work consists of reviewing these impressions and defining our predispositions so that old programming doesn't deviate our energies. In the next section I will outline exercises which will evoke some of these mechanisms so that they can be reprogrammed.

I suggest following the Inner Alchemy vertical alignment and protection practices given later by a review of the day's activities. This is usually best done at night. At this point one may ask (and receive) forgiveness for whatever unconscious, selfish acts or tantrums one may have been subject to during the day. One should review these events impartially but with clarity and positive feeling. This way we disenergize old useless thoughtforms and create space for the future.

When the concrete mind which acts as the guardian of the child cooperates with consciousness, it opens to receive the higher frequencies of true forgiveness. The exercises on the Rhythm of Forgiveness[9] cuts across all the adherences and thought-patterns of the unconscious, through the dynamite of the activated little vortices of the subconscious and through whatever lines of force may be projected onto us.

Christianity maintains, 'By the grace of God you have been forgiven.' Many of us have felt the tremendous peace, light, or electricity that seems to shower over us when we allow ourselves to believe and accept this statement. At those times we open our doors, empty out the programmes of our computer, and connect with Christ within. If we remember our prayers as children we may relive the moments that followed, moments of grace and beauty. The same energies which we had projected above and beyond us returned charged and amplified to comfort us. The figures of angels, Jesus, Mary, the saints or any other images or symbols represent archangelic irradiation and higher order. We know now that they are indeed mirrors, reflections of ourselves.

Through inner alchemical means we are creating a new specie, forging a new physical substance which is malleable, translucid, versatile and strong, strong enough to incorporate the higher voltages of Christ within. This substance is consciousness anchored in physical expression, the new body of Man. Every time we create such a perfect vehicle, its catalyzing radiations bless and transmute everything around, as did the Master Himself in embodying Love.

Chapter Nine

EMBRACING HEAVEN AND EARTH
(Exercises and Meditations)

Centring & Alignment

In our times, old thoughtforms are being dispelled. This trend serves to blend disparate elements together. The centre of operations for this dynamic is within the lower centres. Through the power of organization and integration, the resulting force synthesizes the great pairs of opposites to create a new order. This mechanism rules over death and gives impetus to the entire process of spiritualization. It is the essence of alchemy.

The exercises included in the following sections may bring up latent fears and anxieties, old wounds or impulses directly related to the thoughtforms associated with the lower centres, which obstruct the natural flow of energies as they seek spiritual expression. As one feels the surge of these energies and forces which one has managed to keep at bay, they trigger psychological and bio-physical reactions. It is important not to confuse the intensity of negative reactions which we produce with the primal matrix of force.

In practising awareness, we are asked to remain conscious and centred at the heart. Here there is nothing to do. One's very Being is saturated with the plenitude of life. The contact with the Primal Matrix gives vitality. Our sustained consciousness at the heart refines this into intelligence and love applied creatively in the world. At this moment centring triggers alignment. We avail ourself of the linear modalities to consciously connect and direct concentric force.

This practice allows us to acknowledge others under the same alignment. We begin to trigger the light in another human being by affinity. If truly grounded in ourself, we are able to stay alert to the manipulative and sometimes degrading influence of the lower self. Light serves to bring about true intelligence and discernment. When we recognize the light source in other persons we are in a very real way alleviating their karmic load. This gives them a fresh opportunity to actually change.

Inversely, every time we recall past negative activity in ourselves or in others we reinforce negative conditions.

BASIC PRACTICE: CREATING THE ALCHEMICAL CIRCUIT

First Step: **Reabsorbing projected energies or entering within. Grounding.**

Closing your eyes, become aware as you do so that you are drawing your atom of consciousness within, bringing your focus of attention inside the container of the physical body, noting its contours and occupying the whole area within the skin. Be especially careful to occupy the entire physical space, particularly the legs and feet. Take notice that your body is the Earth. Become grounded in the feeling of it, sensing the security and fertility of the earth within you.

Second Step: **Taking inventory of the elements of the Earth within and distributing awareness evenly inside the vehicle.**

Using the power of your attention to activate the sensory equipment, imagine that your ordinary outer senses are now operating as inner sensors. Sense the weight of your physical body and distribute it evenly, noting where it is heaviest and where it is lightest. This will give you an idea of which parts of the body are densest normally, and which are less inhabited by your awareness.

Scan the entire body from within and now note the delicate complexities of the various elements moving inside you. (When this segment is emphasized, we can self-diagnose imbalances in order to set them right).

Once again, become aware of the whole body but this time look upon it as if it were a mother – Mother Earth. Appreciate the gift of life. Consciously emit gratitude for the precious substance which houses you and lends you all its materials for your use in the development of consciousness.

Sense the physical organism and begin to commune with its subtle pulsations. Note how the pulsing in the pelvic area is different from that in the stomach, the chest, your cheeks... Delight in the inner orchestration of the elements within you, now adding the feeling and sensation of the breath. Progressively expand it, breathing more and more deeply but relaxedly. Be one with the entire physical complex, which will give you sta-bility, security and the basic raw material, as substance and force, which you will use in the development of consciousness.

Third Step: **Igniting the points of light; connecting with the electrical properties within matter.**

Now tune into the points of light within the atomic structure of the physical body, imagining and, with the memory of feeling, sensing how that these points respond by increased electrical charge to your focus upon them. Scan the entire body again, this time from the feet upward, taking special care to feel the ignition of each area at a time. Begin by the feet and travel up the legs, stopping long enough at the knees, then at the pelvic cradle, entering within the sexual area, intestines and other internal organs, bones, muscles... each part responding with the sensation of heightened elec-tricity. Include the skin as well. Once you reach the neck, drop down through the arms and hands and then return to the base of the skull.

Approach the brain as a whole, the three parts of the brain equally lighting into a pale golden hue, billions of points of light scintillating. Take a moment now to allow that move -ment to spread down the spine and through the nervous filaments, charging the body.

Now feel the entire body as one glowing, vibrating body of light... electrically alive. Simultaneously feel the magnetic property of the elements of the body, their density and weight, their texture and fluidity responding to the light frequencies within. Allow and co-participate with the irradiatory property of light as it illumines substance, accel-erating the vibrational rhythm of matter.

Feel yourself as a brilliant, glowing, highly energized body of light, and simultaneous-ly feel yourself as a vigorous, pulsating body of denser matter which lends you securi-ty and solidity – a form. Expanding the activity of light first, then return to a normal state, rest a few seconds and then repeat the cycle, expanding, decreasing, resting... This serves to exercise the light structure and purify elemental matter, lending it more flexibility and in a very real way befriending the intelligence within the cells.

Fourth Step: **Contacting the Central Sun within. Centring.**

Contemplate and commune with the inner microcosm from the perspective of an impartial observer. Marvel at the billions of stars, planets, suns and moons, the currents ebbing and flowing, the vortices spinning and spiralling within the system, and find the central focus of life-giving activity, the Central Sun at the level of the heart centre in the middle of the upper chest[10]. Be sure to use all your senses. Don't rely on your sight only; the most important sense now is feeling.

At this point you might want to take another inventory of the layers within the body, noticing the physical, the emotional and the mental complexes, and how they interact. Train yourself to distinguish them, observing them functioning together, separately, and then together again.

Become especially aware of how your own emotions act upon the entire organism, choosing now to generate joy, happiness, and especially gratitude for the magnificence of creation. Your own feeling of gratitude will intensify the irradiation of the heart ,causing it to shine brighter and to expand. Amplify this by visualizing and feeling the rays from this Central Sun expanding equally in all directions around you.

Pause for a few seconds, or minutes... to enjoy the feeling of fullness, the plenitude of life within. Then direct yourself inwardly to the very core of this great sphere, seeming to travel within concentric space into the heart of creation. Find yourself in the very centre of an enormous field of orgasmic light activity which appears endless and magnificent. Enjoy the goldenness of its irradiation, in fullness and all-one-ness.

Upon returning from your reverie within formlessness, establish a communication with the sun inside, a deep intimacy with your own causal Self, your Christ Self, feeling both loved by it and love for it, in infinite space and yet with a sense of centredness within it. Now you may detect the inner voice within you which affirms 'I AM'.

Silently repeat, 'I AM'... 'I AM'... 'I AM'... Feel this 'Am-ness'... And now feel this 'I'... This 'I' which is not the ordinary you that you know and yet is deeper, truer... Rejoice both in the proximity with infinite space as with the Christ Self... (Remain here for as long as you like.)

Fifth Step: **Aligning. Assuming a position within a body and upon the planet.**

From within the heart chamber extend your awareness now to include your full body. Notice the ray of light which traverses through the body from head to coccyx and out through both legs to pierce the earth underneath you. This gives you a sense of linearity within multi-dimensionality. Notice how the heart is truly the centre of activity for both elemental force and electronic energies. (You may pause here if you like, taking note of the mechanisms of force and energy, of ascending and descending life).

Now direct your attention upward. Be sure to maintain an awareness of the body as a grounding agent, a solid base with its roots upon the earth.[11] As you look upward sense how the electrical circuitry within you, including the points of light, responds with accelerated frequency. Direct yourself upward through the ray which now appears as a beam of life. The upward movement corresponds to increased vibratory frequency at the level of the light body (composed of billions of points of light), leading to greater and greater voltages. Continue to direct your awareness upwards as high as possible.

See the ray emerging from this elevated place and anchored below you in your own heart. Now notice that there is an enormous sphere with concentric orbs of light which reverberate around this glorious and even greater sun source which you are.

Sixth Step: **Linking with Electronic Energies**.

This greater sun is an outpost of monadic energies, what has been termed the divine Presence or the Great 'I AM'. Go right into its centre, just like you did within your heart. Allow yourself to stay there as long as you can, once again partaking of concentric infinity: an infinity within, an infinity without...

When returning, adopt the linear perspective and conceive of the area below you. Imagine that your body is directly connected to yourself as this great sun and direct the joy that you feel at being part of this splendour down into your physical body. Sense the simultaneity of your existence within the body and within this centre of life. Feel the truth behind the affirmation: 'I AM' (here on this Earth, in this body) What 'I AM' in infinite eternity. ' 'I AM' THAT 'I AM'.' Establish the Alchemical Circuit that connects your consciousness with both Earth and heavens. The divine Presence above is a solar presence, identical to the presence within the heart. Maintain both feeling-sensations above and within simultaneously.

Visualize this connection through the light ray only now irradiating into a great tube of light, a gigantic cylinder coming from above, surrounding the body and underneath it like a laboratory test tube. Without losing the connection with the higher outpost, sense the feeling of protection that electronic substance provides around your physical self. Accept and enjoy it. It is real. It is a direct emanation of higher energies and also corresponds to your now more accelerated vibrational level in the body. As long as your physical self is harmonious and vibrating in syntony with the light you are able to sustain this shield.

This part of the practice can also be extended to perceive the different light colorations continuously charging and acting upon the physical self.

Seventh Step: **Heaven and Earth. Here and Now.**

Maintain the awareness of the sourcing of life above you now and the origin of elemental forces below you, meeting within and expressing through you. Be fully in the present moment in your body, with a feeling of centredness here and now, and alignment with cosmic source. If this practice is established, the projection mechanism which creates entanglement through horizontal activity is eventually disenergized.

As human beings who house the light seed within, we possess a tremendous wealth of power which we unfortunately use unconsciously and destructively. This basic practice makes us aware of our connection with the source. It also makes us deeply respectful of the substance of our bodies by reminding us of our commitment with the elements. We use visualization and feeling to activate inner senses and affirm our choice to identify with light rather than with lower human creation. This light is not opposed to matter; it is the very heart of it. Lower human creation, on the other hand, is the very ugliness of sub- or unconscious astral activity. Instead of using the body to serve us, honouring it, and taking good care of it, we drive it to excesses. At emotional and mental levels, instead of tuning into universal mind, we identify with collective thought formations, losing awareness of the monadic source, which like a still, small voice within recalls, 'I AM'....

Our every act, thought and feeling here declares our godliness. Elemental intelligence follows our orders. In recognizing our source and in affirming that we stand united with the light centred in the heart, we draw from the authority of that light. In this way we speak, think, act and feel with the power from the Father, with the full cooperation from the Mother as the matrix of space and the source of elemental force. Our management of elemental life becomes sacrosant. These very forces then serve consciousness instead of engendering and feeding unconsciousness.

THE ALCHEMICAL CIRCUIT

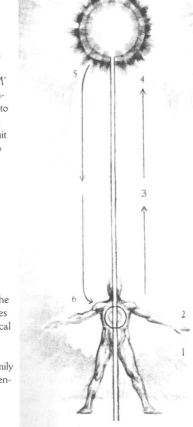

5. The conscious projection emanating from the perspective of the 12th dimensional 'I AM' towards the 3rd dimensional 'I' which serves to pierce through realities and complete the circuit initiated at the 3rd step indicated above: the answer.

4. Cosmic identity: the act of feeling oneself one with the fountain of Life or the individual divine essence. Fusion.

3. the invocation or directional act of energetic acceleration: the call which evokes the answer.

6. The acceptance. The incorporation of realities both cosmic and physical in simultaneous fusion with the Self which includes the whole family of Self in its multi-dimensionality.

2. The focusing or consciousness stimulation of the heart centre as an identity point and a meeting place of cosmic energies constituting a replica of the 12th dimensional 'I AM' in matter.

1. The awakening of the points of light in the centre of the physical atoms of the entire body, which as whole compose the body of light. This is a process through which one becomes aware both of the weight of matter and of the electricity of the subtle body, culminating in the creation of a physical anchor: grounding.

Through the Alchemical Circuit we redirect unconscious horizontal involvement into conscious vertical dimensions of causality, resulting in better relationships. The following illustrations show how this dynamic works in direct proportion to our inner posture.

VERTICAL VS. HORIZONTAL LINKING I

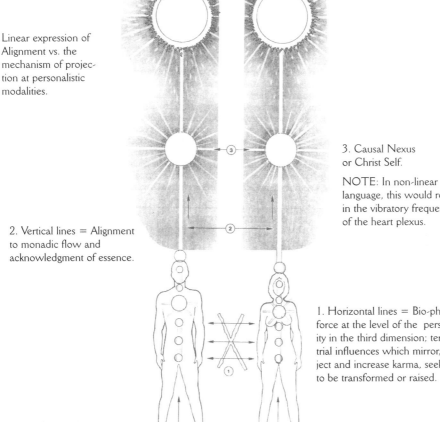

Linear expression of Alignment vs. the mechanism of projection at personalistic modalities.

3. Causal Nexus or Christ Self.

NOTE: In non-linear language, this would reflect in the vibratory frequency of the heart plexus.

2. Vertical lines = Alignment to monadic flow and acknowledgment of essence.

1. Horizontal lines = Bio-physical force at the level of the personality in the third dimension; terrestrial influences which mirror, project and increase karma, seeking to be transformed or raised.

A third application of the golden substance of light is done at the level of the 'hara', that terrific powerhouse which marks the meeting of fire and water on the body. Here we may visualize, and actually collect energy as a ball of light at the frontal part of the navel.

Take the time to gather these energies into a buddha-belly around the navel. Sense the ball and qualify it with golden frequency. Now turn it around, first clockwise, then counterclockwise, then towards the front and lastly toward the spine. Each round should consist of eight revolutions. This martial arts practice anchors us on the earth. The belly draws from the vitality reserves of the earth through your own body in a centring practice that will naturally ground you and redistribute your energies so that they can be used for maximum clarity and efficacity in the world.

Listening with the Feet

Walking in the Master's footsteps alludes to a life lived in imitation of Christ, only that people neglect to notice that footsteps means feet. Most of us are disconnected from our feet and many people don't really like their feet. In fact, most feet are ugly and distorted. This suggests that our contact with the earth is also distorted.

Feet are the natural absorbers and dischargers of energy. Energy is best discharged through the feet which channel the excess into the earth, where it is recycled. We absorb magnetism and vitality from the earth through different portions of the soles of the feet which relate to diverse energy centres and meridians. The very outermost heel portion corresponds to the second chakra. A bit further in, still on the heel, corresponds to the first. The centre portion under the arch relates to the third, whereas the ball of the foot activates the fourth. The section pertaining to the fifth chakra is right under the toes on the fleshy part, while the third eye area is reflected under the big toe. The part at the end of the big toe under the nail stimulates the seventh centre.

The following practice is a variant of a popular '70's exercise and heightens full body awareness. It is done in a relaxed, natural setting. The key will be in the selection of the musical piece which should be melodious and deeply resonating. I have found that string instruments work best.

Lie with your feet towards the speakers and attune yourself to the sensitivity at the soles of the feet. Transfer your faculty of hearing there in order to detect the fine ondulations and vibrations of the music through the termination of the energy meridians at the soles of the feet, becoming sensitive to and absorbing the waves coming from the sound.

As a first stage allow the music to simply flow into you, filling your entire body with harmonious waves that tingle and trickle upwards like a delicate streaming through the nerves and conduits of the body. Follow the currents upwards through the subtle networks in the innermost parts of the body. (When this practice is done with colour visualization to accompany the music, violet flame streaming is used from the feet upwards. In the opposite direction, once the flow has been established from the bottom up, liquid golden light is used to soothe the antiseptic intensity of violet).

Once the body is saturated with these streamings, which build up a keen inner sensitivity, the process becomes one of circulating the energies within the body. Now the hands are used to irradiate the energies, opening up the small chakras in the palms of the hand: the male participant raises his right hand from the elbow; the female participant her left hand. The music entering through the soles of the feet is sent into the world through the indicated palm. Now raise both hands and allow one hand to receive and the other to irradiate. Sense this irradiation activity and the flow up through the body. When absorbing the sound frequencies through the hand, the streaming crosses into and through the heart and out through the irradiating palm.

The next stage marks a vaster irradiatory activity. This time you raise your entire arm to irradiate into the universe at a higher level of frequency.

At the last stage you use your fingertips to funnel energies into the different chakras or body centres. The feet and legs are considered part of the base chakra. The music is now channeled into the belly at the navel, feeding the second and third centres at the point of maximum benefit. Fill the navel with these streamings, whirling and swirling within, collecting and gathering, soothing and centring awareness in that place.

After a few minutes bring the hands up to the heart centre and delight with the harmonies produced at the level of the heart. Allow the central sun there to absorb and magnify the sound frequencies in all directions. After a while funnel the music into the area of the third eye where an inner bathing and subtle activation occurs as the belly, heart and third eye blend into one unit. You may like to place one hand on the belly and the other on the centre of the forehead, or you may want to take the energies right through the body again, this time focussing on the top of the head at the seventh chakra. Return to the belly and end at the heart centre. You may wish to return to other areas in between.

This meditation does wonders for the body which delights in harmony and expands the activity of the points of light to blend with the streams. It raises the vibration in a delicate way that integrates matter with light. It also fosters sensitivity and promotes awareness of energy circulation: two important ingredients for conscious relating.

The Microcosmic Orbit

Our bio-physical energies normally leak out through the genitals, the eyes, ears, nose and mouth, as well as through our emotions and our thoughts, or they build up into intense pressure in the head or create innumerable stomach and intestinal disorders.

THE MICROCOSMIC ORBIT

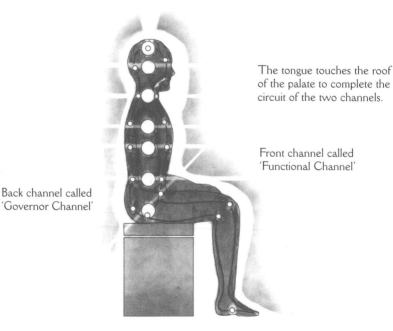

The tongue touches the roof of the palate to complete the circuit of the two channels.

Front channel called 'Functional Channel'

Back channel called 'Governor Channel'

Visualizing the body circuits in this practice we are able to clear the physical and mental blockages and process a greater amount of elemental force. We gradually induce the atom of consciousness from its position within the heart centre to draw the energy at the base of the spine up safely and naturally. As the energy circulates, it not only revitalizes all parts of the mind and body but it becomes sealed within the body.

The major paths used by Taoists for the circulation of this energy through the body are especially strong currents which curve the front and back parts of the body. They are called the 'functional channel' and the 'governor channel'. Widely known by the science of acupunture, these channels link up the key centres throughout the body. The 'functional channel' begins at the base of the trunk midway between the penis or vagina and the anus at the perineum, curving upwards through the abdominal organs, the heart and throat to end at the tip of the tongue. The 'governor channel' starts in the same place but flows from the perineum upwards through the tail bone and up through the spine into the brain and curving back down to the roof of the mouth.

> Identify bio-physical energy, distinguishing it from subtle light currents. Now mentally circulate the energy beginning at the level of the palate, bringing the flow down the front through the tongue, throat, chest and navel, then down and around the tailbone and spine back up to the head. In order to connect the two channels at the mouth, you should place your tongue tip at the front of the roof of the mouth and keep it there.

> Guide the energy up the outer part of the spine (not through the spine),and down the front creating an ellipse or orbit. At first you may not feel as if much is happening. Gently and steadily continue, persisting regularly with loving intentionality. Energy will respond to your call in time.

Whereas electronic energy is sensed electrically through amplitude, elemental force (or bio-energy) is perceived as a denser, slower flow. The circulation in the Microcosmic Orbit is meant to facilitate the flow of the thicker, heavier bio-physical energies which promote vitality. The practice of the Alchemical Circuit, by contrast, aims at linking one up with finer energies from the heavens and earth. Both are essential elements within the work of Inner Alchemy. These two basic practices lay the groundwork for all work which aims at integrating matter and light, heaven and earth, male and female within, concentricity and linearity, activity and receptivity, illumination and practical action in the world.

Breathing Awareness

A simple way of restoring balance and simultaneously discovering ourself through the body is conscious breathing. Directing your breath with awareness through your body is equivalent to directing your atttention (your atom of consciousness) to the living cells from the vantage point of the heart. It is a wonderful way of discovering the different parts of your body and communicating with them, taking them under your direct wing so to speak, and co-participating with them in the process of life.

> The essence behind an activity which leads into meditation is the quality of intent, coupled with unitary feeling and sensation, which builds up 'momentum'. If so inclined, keep a rhythm and set a time for being with yourself.

> As you breathe, play with the different kinds, rhythms and parts of your breathing. Experiment releasing the flow through the legs, hands... Give yourself enough time to see, listen to, feel and integrate the energies. See what they are saying to you. Allow yourself to remember and associate. Recorded music of Tibetan monks chanting those deeply resonant sounds that reverberate in the innermost recesses of your cells can enhance your experience greatly.

> You may come face to face with major blocks at the psychological or body level which obstruct full orgasmic participation with life. The breath must courageously go hand in hand with let go and awareness. It is a new experience of contact with life at the level of the body's memories and perceptions.

> The body and the chakras work as a unit. If one is a bit off, the others will follow suite or compensate for the malfunction in some way. A disequilibrium engendered by the centres triggers off a similar imbalance in the corresponding energetic body around and within the physical. This dynamic also manifests around the external environment of the individual, affecting people and events — wife, children, financial situation and professional performance.

In this light we can understand the psychology triggering frigidity, insatisfaction, homosexuality and the root causes of fanaticism (second chakra), competition (third chakra), asceticism (second chakra), thrillseeking (first and third chakras) and prejudice (fourth chakra). Medical doctors and psychiatrists would do well to study their own internal dynamics in order to best help their fellow men through the readjustment of what are basically energetic imbalances in the psycho-physical network. The frightening truth is that practically everyone today is operating from a debilitated system contaminated both at organic and psychological levels.

Meditation on Mother Earth and Father Heaven

Lie down carefully releasing your body on the floor as if you were lying down upon the lap of the Mother. It is important that you put aside whatever psychological reactions you may have with your physical mother and tune into the Supreme Eternal Mother, perfect femininity both earthly and sublime. Feel the contact with the earth. (If you can do this on the bare earth, even better.) Feel the reciprocal pulsating in your own body as you surrender completely to the pulsing breast of the great Mother. Relax within this intimacy.

Become aware of the breath which, like a wave, forms an elliptical orbit, deep, relaxed, slow and full, in... out... without pause or holding. Work up to this slow rhythm, letting go of all physical tension, increasing and widening the breath without forcing it. As you breathe in, imagine that you are absorbing light from the sun and that that light flows into and activates all the points of light in the body. On the outbreath, imagine that the breath is being released through the pores of the body evenly, as the points of light radiate more intensely.

Inbreath, a taking-in of life from the sun; outbreath, radiating the points of light and expelling the air through every pore of the body.

Affirm your commitment to the light with the breathing, inviting and calling for more light to enter within each cell of your body. Remain aware and command the body to relax continuously. You will be aware of two activities within the body: at the level of dense elemental matter and at the level of electrical charge. Allow solar energy to meet with matter within. Keep the mouth open and the jaw relaxed. Breathe deeply through the mouth into every cell and atom. Delight with this communion inside you.

Assume full responsibility for your body on earth. This is your personal territory, your planet. Go deeply into its heart now, deeply inside yourself to find the heart of the Mother. Don't direct it to any particular place in the body yet, simply reach that innermost sanctuary where you may find Her. It is a soft sinking feeling within, a relishing

Chapter Ten

FIRE INTO LIGHT

Lusting after things, persons, power or self-importance is the product of horizontal chakra activity in the lower triad, while pure and right desire, when intense and one-pointed, moves us out of the range of the unconscious addictive, claiming egoism. But there is much suffering before the emotional nature is cleansed and the driving fire-force of consciousness is developed.

It is important at this point that we do not swing from the passionate attachment and involvement of the lower centres to the indifference and callousness which is sometimes enforced when the heart centre opens and its serenity provokes a very real cooling of the lower fires. The process which follows is delicate and sensitive. As part of our karmic cleaning we review the accumulated instinctual and physical reactions of humanity encoded within us.

In the East it is said that the person is like a candle burning at both ends now. We have converted the vitality provided by the element fire to ignite the fire of consciousness which triggers the activity of another, higher correlate, the white fire of the heart. In the chamber of the heart, the white fire no longer burns as combustion; it illumines in the sense of light. There is a great difference between the lower chakra psychic heat and the spiritual warmth of true light, as fire itself transmutes into light.

The process at the solar plexus, the fire centre of human consciousness, is tricky and dual. On the one hand the work must be approached through the igniting of the heart. The awakening and quickening of the chakras will follow suite in relative safety. On the other hand, we cannot gain the full intuitional light produced by the heart modality unless we have integrated the lessons of impeccability dictated by the solar plexus. This centre provides an essential power force in true human alchemy that we need to understand.

The heart centre is considered the central sun of our microcosm. It illumines, nourishes and catalyzes the entire process of redemption. This is more a symbolic and poetic image than a dynamic one. Energetically, the solar plexus is the central sun power for the lower bodies. At a later stage the third eye functions as a central sun for spirit. Balanced spiritual sight occurs when the two functional suns, the solar plexus and the third eye, are united. For this reason ancient shamanic traditions placed such emphasis upon its integration.

A master is one who has the solar plexus wheel emanating as a pure white sun. This centre is a major body brain, a planetary radar for the lower bodies. It contains the physical powers of emanation, radiation, illumination and animation. We must master the third chakra before using these powers of consciousness relating to the higher self in the causal modality. In its primitive state this centre is a fiery contracting and expanding master-pulse automatically triggering the vagus nerve[12] behind the navel, to stimulate the heat-generating mechanism of the second chakra. In its higher aspects it flows to feed the 'hara', igniting a master primal (white light) healing centre in conjunction with the refined forces of the second chakra.

The science of yoga arose as a way of providing training in the use of physical energies by utilizing mantrams, breathing and visualizations which gather, remould and redirect heat. The psychic powers acquired by the seeker are actually the result of a deep dynamic at the level of the solar plexus. These powers are the product of chakra integration but they also present a temptation to the person who must use them only for the development of consciousness. The 'hara' as a mediation station serves to generate heat, while also making it possible to resist the astral current existing in the emotional and sensation life, by providing real grounding. The science of yoga arose as a way of providing training in the use of physical energies by utilizing mantrams, breathing and visualizations which gather, remould and redirect heat.

The solar plexus is both a sending and receiving station for all the chakras. The power to send effective blessings (or the opposite) flows forth from this centre. Hostile emanations and radiations begin here. Fear, the basic emotion on which all negative emotions are rooted, moves against it, leaving a knot or sinking feeling within the pit of the stomach which acts upon the hormone system and causes astral poisons.

For those of us who must learn to master lust, for example, someone will incite our lusting. If we are trying to be free of revenge or retaliation, someone will reflect our hatreds. If sloth is our problem we will be confronted by our own resentment. If we are proud we will surely trip in our own arrogance. And if doubt clouds our thinking, we may never really see the light. Life itself seeks resolution, a resolution obtained only through the integrating power of the solar plexus.

Once the solar plexus is activated and brought into direct participation within the process of consciousness, its controlling and supervisory abilities are energetically transferred over to the secondary centre at the navel. This insight earns us the understanding of why the 'hara' has played such a vital role in Eastern esoteric tradition for millenia.

The next exercise has to do with the invocation of light qualified with the properties of the violet coloured ray and might truly be considered an alchemical practice of the highest order when performed under conditions of utmost sincerity and impeccable one-pointedness. It requires of the person only that he be honest with himself. What makes the sucess of the exercise is right intent. The process consists in dissolving the lines of force that link us compulsively to individuals. The seriousness behind this simple practice marks the extent of its depth.

> The most important part of this exercise consists in your preparation for it. While in a meditative state of introspection you will need to answer a few questions. Examine your desire-nature, the motivations and relationships you have had with persons at the physical and emotional levels of involvement.

> As explained previously, particularly where there has been an exchange of sexual fluids, horizontal links crystallize into cord-like passages that conduct astral currents between people, creating very real conduits of force. When there is no real or deep commitment these conduits serve to tie people together in game-playing projections. We literally give away portions of our autonomy, power, independence, intelligence and substance to the other, buying the other and selling ourself in order to have our 'needs' met.

> I would like to propose that you reconsider just what the implicit conditions behind each of your major relationships are, to uncover the fundamental dynamics involved and the role each actually plays in your life and personality. Now ask yourself if you are willing to break that kind of tie with the other. Take enough time to consider what your life would be like without that particular gestalt that feeds your relationship. If there are conditionals in your answer, then I suggest not performing the exercise. It will be better to wait for another time.

> You need to decide this on your own without the coerction of your friends or partner. Only you are involved, even if you are in a committed relationship. Your inward journey does not depend on whether your partner agrees or not. If both parties want

to do the exercise side by side, although laudable and helpful for a fresh start, it does not add any merit. The exercise is done alone in deep and solitary communion with the higher self and through the electronic voltage of monadic response to your call. It is at times and in exercises such as this that you begin to see just how transitory and essentially superficial our human relationships are when compared to that greater relationship with life.

Now make a list of all your difficult (painful, embarassing, guilt-ridden) relationships at physical and emotional levels. This means relationships that involve manipulation. Unfortunately however, this exercise cannot dissolve the karma within blood relationships which are based on stronger bonds and often unknown motivations.

Once you have made your list then you must review the conditions and circumstances, the feelings and thoughts that went into feeding that relationship, with as vivid detail as possible. You will be summoning up all the physical, emotional and mental energies that constructed those voluntary links with the other. If it was a long affair, then review a number of characteristic moments.

Try and remember even that one-time person you had sex with at the office party when you got drunk, or that other 'accident' when you couldn't stop yourself. Especially if it was done in unconsciousness or compulsion, review the mechanisms of your feeling-experience. You exchanged precious vital fluids which are essentially an aspect of primordial light and relate to creation. Although it may not seem as serious when we just carry on extended flirtations without sex, consider also what kind of creations you loosed at the psychological level. Ask yourself if you want to live with them. As a custodian of elemental life and as a channel for cosmic energies you are responsible for much more than your little personal self.

Burning Karma

As we are dealing with the use of elemental substance and force in this exercise, add to your initial meditation the contact with Mother Earth.

Feel the embrace of Mother Earth supporting you as you relax deeply upon the ground on your back. Feel the synchronicity of your living tissue with the heartbeat of the Earth. Connect with the body of humanity through you and with profound humility ask forgiveness from your Self, from the Mother... from the archangelic regents of elemental intelligence, and from the people you have involved in your unconsciousness.

As we enter into the invocation of the violet flame and set up the atmosphere for the exercise to follow, allow the words spoken to be your own, the feeling generated to be your feeling... Visualize and sense the violet flame surrounding and saturating your body, knowing that this frequency represents your harmonious potential aligned with higher purpose. Acknowledge the Presence within your heart and radiating above you as the source of your life, your love, your intelligence, and the only power present in creation. In this way unite and identify yourself with the Father-Mother God in the name and authority of the Son.

When performing this ritual you may tape my words in your own voice and use it as a guided meditation, leaving all the time that you need at the end to approach each person, each case carefully and conscientiously, sensing and feeling the lines of force that unite you with the other, tenderly withdrawing your energies from the thoughtform and seeing the energies of the other returning to them. You will do this while visualizing the scene in question clearly (animated with the feelings that you have invested and which you have recalled), as a scene on celluloid tape. You will then witness the tape(s) burning to a crisp and dissolving the thoughtform. You must say the name of the person out loud and in this way evoke the higher self aspect of the person with whom you are attuned. You should have placed the person within the same Alchemical Alignment as yourself, recognizing God in him or her with profound respect.

Try Gregorian or Tibetan music for this process. The resonance created by the chant of monks seems to create just the right atmosphere. You will be burning the energetic complex which represents unconsciousness and in no way harming anyone. Your essential relationship here is with the principle of perfection, the Human Prototype.

Invocation:

'We affirm the Presence of light as the only Presence acting in our world, in our bodies and in this atmosphere. (Say or think this with power and conviction.)

We call upon the presence of the angels of the violet transmuting flame which purifies and dissolves in order to restore the natural order and sanctity of life. We also call upon the Lords of Karma to assist us in our endeavour...'

'Assuming responsability for our faculties and the substance of our bodies we entrust ourselves to the activity of the violet ray through the violet flame action.

In the name of the Presence which "I Am", we accept the activity of the violet flame within and through us, illumining and purifying our physical, emotional and mental vehicles.'

'We are grateful for this opportunity of being able to return to each of our partners the energies and forces which we accepted and ask during this consumption process that all residual energy, substance and thought-form of the past and present, including all destructive akashic records be dissolved.

We invoke the mighty "I AM" Presence and higher self of each of our partners, and in the name of the presence which is light, which is love, which is truth, we ask for the liberation from all the effects of our unconscious acts.'

'The angels of the blue ray surround us as a protective wall, cutting and dissolving any lines of force which could come as a result of the dissolution of our ties in this moment.

Centred within the heart as the expression of our higher self in this dimension we affirm light. Our world is now saturated with light.'

'We now invoke the individual Self and higher mental body of _____ (name of the person), and with deep appreciation for his/her presence in this world we ask his/her permission to act upon the forms which we have jointly created.' (Visualize the person, circumstances, emotions and sensations, intensifying the memory... now!)

Awaken that etheric feeling-memory within your bodies, visualizing and feeling intensely the presence of the other, relaxing your own body and opening the deep inner spaces within. Visualize and feel... without judgement... sense the lines of force which are connected with your own body. See where they are and focus upon them.

(Say individually:) 'In the name and authority of my Presence and in the name and authority of the Presence of _____ (name of the person), through the Power of our Lord and Master, Jesus Christ, we accept the activity of the angels of the violet flame, the salamanders of the etheric fire, and all Beings of light that they may dissolve these thoughtforms, impressions, registers and memories with the sacred transmuting fire'.

Now visualize the celluloid film and watch the burning, burning, burning of it... Burning the forms slowly, deeply, totaly. Burning... loosening the lines of force from your body and placing them into the violet flame... Burning, burning, burning... pulling forth and out of the lower centres... Burning and dissolving, dissolving, dissolving... becoming ashes... And dissolving the adherences in our physical bodies, observe that the transmuted energies which belong to us return from the other person now purified, and the energies which we accepted from the other now return to the other person. Thank them for the life lesson.

Now you invoke a second person following the same procedure as for the first. Stay with the process for as long as you need to, careful not to tire yourself. You can always finish at another time following the same sequence.

The next exercise focuses upon the building energies of the three primary rays which comprise the Three-Fold Flame. This Three-Fold Flame is in essence our Essence; its invocation and visualization harmonizes and balances us. This is followed by a meditation on the Five-Pointed Star, a means of incorporating and integrating the positive attributes possible to Man.

Lastly, 'Seeing Beyond Karma: On the Plane of Truth'; concerns itself with developing the ability to see beyond our expectations and corresponds to accepting the basic experiences with our parents as necessary lessons in true forgiveness and transcendence.

The Three-Fold Flame

If you have difficulty visualizing colour, I suggest you buy gift-wrapping paper in metallic royal blue, deep pink, and bright gold. Familiarize yourself with the shades first, then trust that you have imbibed the frequencies which you will transpose into the heart in this meditation.

After Alignment and Centring:

Visualize the Three-Fold Flame in the centre of the heart chakra in the middle of
the chest. (Actually, this phenomenon is the result of a perfect alignment or overlapping of each of the bodies of the personality, which is represented by each colour).

The Three-Fold Flame sprouts from the heart centre in three colours, blue for the
Father on your right, yellow-gold in the centre for the Son, and deep pink representing the Holy Spirit or matrix on your left. Allow this image to trigger the feeling and
sensation within the heart which irradiates in all directions a fine golden glow.

Now focussing on the rich, deep blue flame, allow it to spread up to your right
shoulder and descend down your right arm, expanding and spreading out through
your fingers, falling like a plumed streaming onto the floor beneath your feet. See the
streaming igniting and expanding over your entire right side, now glowing brightly
from the right side of the spine and diminishing at an angle which covers your right
arm like a great wing of glorious blue with crystal silver speckles.

Feel the quality of this deep, rich blueness and enjoy the frequency of pure power
and strength that the Father aspect brings to you. Go directly inside that feeling.
From the left side of your heart centre now sense the deep pink flame growing and
spreading up to the left shoulder and down the left arm, streaming down your fingertips onto the floor and igniting into pink flames over your entire left side, from the
spine to and including the right arm.

Feel and absorb the beauty and the qualities of love, abundance and deep joy that
this frequency gives you... an intense ecstatic peace which sparkles like golden stars
within the pink! Remain with that feeling until you absorb it through the entire
blood-stream, as the pink winglike formation continues to glow on your left side.

Now direct your attention to the golden flame in the centre of the heart and feel the
golden-yellow Christ flame of love-wisdom and illumination, of intelligence and universal love rising up to the throat, beyond your face, illumining your eyes, your brain
and your entire mental field and bursting into flame above your head from where it
continues to reach for the heavens.

Sense the golden flame irradiating, awakening, accelerating the vibratory frequency in the brain, attuning it to higher Mind... And now allow it to spread downwards as well, like a pillar of golden flames from head to toe. Imbibe that feeling, that frequency which regenerates and illumines.

Now... as the golden pillar of light flows through you, lengthening you, allowing you to feel at one with the Presence above and within you... sense the three flames' activity simultaneously. Hold that image and feeling for a while.

Allowing the golden flame to remain as a radiant axis within and through you, now observe the pink and blue flames merging beneath your feet and see the violet flame birthing... sprouting forth and spreading... surrounding your body now with a glorious column of violet fire.

Sense the frequency of the violet flame as it swirls, whirls, explodes, sweeps, boils and blazes through you... Purifying, cleaning, absorbing and transmuting all negative thought-forms, forces, energies, or adherences in your physical, mental, emotional bodies...

Accept this powerful, majestic fire as a continuous activity through your inner and outer world and now let it enter deep within your bones, the blood, and all the cells of your body, refining and preparing you for the encounter with the perfection of light!

Feel your body of light coming alive from within the innermost recesses of your physical body, one and simultaneously with it. A body of light, a body of matter... the violet fire... and the Three-Fold Flame in the heart, eternal, present glory.

As the violet recedes or neutralizes, notice that the Three-Fold Flame surrounds you always and whenever you think of it.

The Five-Pointed Star

This meditation was inspired by Alice Bailey's work.

The upright five-pointed star is the symbol of true humanity, representing not only the five extremities, but also very real lines of magnetic force which the human energy field produces. In magic, the visualization of this star around you is enough to cut through negative elemental lines of force and protect you.

In this meditation five persons are placed in a circle, each one embodying a humane principle. Each person should consider deeply, both mentally and emotionally, the following concepts which he or she will represent physically, mentally and emotionally: peace, cooperation, participation, unity and honesty. As each person generates the qualities inherent in those concepts, he is to gaze into the left eye of the person before him, creating an energetic link or line of force which will combine to form a star. Prepare yourself for the meditation by choosing one concept among the five:

* Peace in the World
* Cooperation with the divine plan for Humanity
* Participation with the divine plan set by Hierarchy
* Unity as a product of the Christ Spirit of brotherly love among men
* Honesty, as you place yourself in the true humbled context of your humanity

CIRCULATION: THE FIVE-POINTED STAR

Once aligned and centred and absorbed by the concept of your choice, sit in a circle with the other four participants. Take a few moments to join hands as you join in purpose. Visualize a ruby-red rose in the centre, a symbol of perfect devotion and human love. Surround your circle with a jointly visualized ring-pass-not of indigo blue to seal your energies and preserve them.

As you open your eyes, gaze softly and unfocussedly into the left eye of person nr. 3 in the chart. Person nr. 3 gazes into the left eye of person nr. 5. Person nr. 5 into the left eye of nr. 2. Nr. 2 into the left eye of nr. 4. And person nr. 4 gazes into your left eye in position nr. 1.

Identify yourselves with humanity, knowing that the number five also represents the perfect master and matter as the vehicle of man. Link yourself as the Son of the Mother-Father of the universe, centred in the heart.

Conceive of the beauty of the planet Earth: the verdant-greens of trees and hills and valleys and orchards... the multicoloured nuances of flowers and vegetation.... the blue-green of the oceans, rivers and lakes... the white of snow... consider the birds and fish, the animals in the wild... the colouring of dawn and dusk... Visualize the planet Earth in all its splendour and magnificence, perfect, clean, where illumined humanity lives in syntony with the laws of nature and the cosmos. Allow the symbol of the rose to arise out of the centre of the earth bursting into fraternal, universal love. Allow your bodies to become golden with the glow of universal love within your heart colouring every cell and fibre... now linking to create an exquisite golden star! Embody light in mind, body and emotion. Become a true child of the light and through the exercise of your free will now join in the spirit of joy and enthusiasm to actualize the essential truth: we are one in the Presence which 'I AM'!

Now open your eyes as windows of your heart and generate the feeling - attribute while visualizing the possibilities of your concept, gazing into the eyes of the person before you. Sustain that eye contact and remain still. Allow that momentum to build and build over fifteen minutes or longer if you can sustain it. Irradiating light... peace... cooperation... participation... unity... honesty...

Generating light... expanding through the earth and from the Earth into the heavens... We are grateful to serve as channels for divine light, perfect and harmonious. Peace to all on earth! Free, joyful, harmonious cooperation! Dynamic, vital participation!

Unity, as the children of Man... I AM' One with them! Expressing the supreme, sub-lime truth of Absolute Infinity.'

Without breaking the links you may end your meditation affirming:

I AM THE LIGHT, THE POWER AND THE GLORY! PERFECT LOVE MANIFESTS THROUGH ME IN THE FULFILMENT OF THE DIVINE PLAN.

Close your eyes softly in the knowledge that this is so.

Seeing Beyond Karma: On the Plane of Truth

This is a guided fantasy inspired from a practice created by my friend Phylliss Moline. Practices such as these are used to create a safe, beautiful space inside, where you can truly be your Self. It is a lengthy process. The individual should allow as much time as possible, pausing in the spaces between images to absorb the potent forces invoked and permit them to reach their destination.

It is a grave mistake to rush out of meditation without allowing for the time needed by your energies to settle and your bodies integrate what has happened. If you do not have time to give yourself afterwards, it is best not to do the practice. This applies to all exercises and meditations.

You will be working with powerful symbology for patriarchal and matriarchal archetypes as embodied through your own parents. You will get nowhere without first having accepted, integrated, forgiven and healed your parents in you – both of them. Everywhere you go they are a force within you, in your very heartbeat and cellular structure, and in your mental and emotional behaviour patterns. Feeling sorry for yourself because you feel you didn't have the kind of parents that you wanted, becoming angry, sour or revengeful, or even trying to ignore them simply doesn't work!

This may be shocking news for some of you but sixty percent of your bodies' materials came from your mother; the remaining forty percent from your father. In some Eastern traditions this proportion is 80/20. Where will you go without them? This is the primary reason why in some monastaries in the East, written permission is required to admit a full grown man or woman into the order. If the mother does not agree to her son's intention, her psychic influence will disturb the sacred atmos-

loved and accepted there; in fact, it really feels like 'home'! This is the plane where your higher self lives. Knowing without knowledge, feel yourself in truth. You notice that this planet is a replica of the Earth only brighter, cleaner, the colours and textures more vivid, clearer and translucid. There is a soft smell of ozone in the air. Everything seems made of crystal, and there is a crystal resonance to the air.

Slowly make your way into a path that leads towards your truth. Remember what this path looks and feels like, as it seems that you have been this way before. Notice what you see along the way, giving yourself permission to feel all the emotions clearly, without confusion, or the veils which normally cloud your perception upon the earth. Entering into and through the scenery, observe a particular tree that attracts your attention. Come close to that tree and in your way try to befriend it. What are the impressions coming from that tree? What kind of tree is it? What do you do, if anything?

Leaving the tree now, continue your pilgrimage to a body of water and allow the first image to remain. What is that body of water? Is it a river, a lake, an ocean, a waterfall, or is it a little stream? Is it deep, or shallow? Get close to it. Enter inside it to find a comfortable large rock that seems to be placed there so that you can sit on it. Place yourself there surrounded by water. Breathe deeply in your body of light and take in the whole atmosphere, what you see, what you feel. Know that it is true.

Now observe in the distance a male figure approaching. Let yourself become interested by this figure which approaches you steadily. As he comes closer and you are able to see his features you will know that it is your father. He may not look exactly like your father, but you know that it is him. How is he dressed? When he comes right in front of you, let yourself look deeply into his eyes, as you also become aware of the emotions which begin to surface, surprising you almost. Know that these are the records impressed upon your emotional body. Allow the sentiments to be there without identifying with them.

What do your father's eyes seem to be saying? Look closely. Take care to recognize his inner Presence as well. As he stands silently before you take in who he is at both personality and higher self levels. Now tune into the source above you that is your own and ask, from the bottom of your heart, to be bathed, redeemed, liberated – both of you. Visualize a mighty ray of coloured light beaming down upon each of you there. A pure colour frequency that emanates from the Self. Observe your father's face and body being showered with this redeeming light, revealing the essential truth about him... about you in regard to him... Ask that this light heal your father, and also yourself, of any past wounds...

Take note of the colour of the ray being sent to you both and know that it is perfect; it cleans and nourishes your father... and you. Observe how his features begin to change, perhaps one face after another begins to reveal itself before your heart's eye. As the light diminishes, look once again into his eyes. What do they seem to be saying now? Take note of all the subtleties of emotion, knowing that everything revealed is in the highest interest: transmuting, healing, forgiving and revealing this deep and essential relationship. As you look at him, each time more deeply, repeat mentally, 'I accept myself'... 'I accept myself'... 'I accept myself'... Knowing without knowledge, liberate your father who has already liberated you upon this Planet of Truth, and let him recede into the distance from where he came. (You may want to pause here in stillness and silence. Make a mental note to remember or communicate now everything you perceive.)

From another place, in the distance appears a female figure. As she approaches you, you notice that she is your mother. How is she dressed? How does she appear? What are her gestures? What does she seem to be saying with her eyes? Recognize this female figure as your mother with all her imperfections and all the hidden beauty within her. Acknowledge your relationship with her and allow yourself to feel her deeply without losing yourself in that feeling. Take in what she seems to be requesting from you...From your heart now, calling for the ultimate good of both, ask for the truth to be revealed within you. See and feel the higher self aspect of your mother and your own. And, from within a source-point above, observe a glorious healing ray descending over you both. See this great cascade luminously purifying and healing her, penetrating deeply within her body... and yours. Each wave of light floods you with healing love. Feel it. Breathe into your body and let it dissolve, redeem, liberate and illuminate the truth within this relationship. Mentally say, 'I forgive myself for being in this relationship'. Repeat this three times, each time feeling it profoundly.

Observe the light washing, transmuting the body and the features of your mother, revealing her essence and the lessons in this relationship... knowing without knowledge with the wisdom of the heart. As the light becomes absorbed, look again into her eyes and recognize the truth. Free her and feel yourself freed from her, allowing her to dissolve into the horizon from where she appeared. (Again, pause here to give yourself time to take in what has happened. You may continue to see a succession of images and experience different emotions. Communicate now or make a mental note to remember it all).

A profound peace descends upon you. You decide to leave the rock and the body of water and make your way back through the path in another direction.
You will now summon an important figure in your life, preferably your husband or your wife, the partner in your life. If you are single, or if your partner is no longer an active influence in your life, call upon your son or daughter, if you have one. It must be one person only. If you have no children, then let it be your best and closest friend or teacher. Evoke the image of this person within you. As he or she appears before you, invite him on a journey.

Before setting out on your journey, let yourself play with this person. Imagine that this person is five years old and that you are the age you are presently. What happens to your relationship? How would you treat this child? What would you say to him? How would this child respond to you? What games would you play?
Now change roles. He is an adult and you are five years old. what would this relationship be like? What games would you play? How? Knowing without knowledge, feeling intensely without losing your heart's clarity, allow both of you to be five years old. Now notice what games you would play and how each of you would act. What is said and what happens now?

Allow yourself to return to your present age and let the other person remain as a five-year old child, as you set off on that journey which now takes you to a cavern. Invite the child into the dark cavern and observe his reaction. He will not want to go into it. In fact he will be adamant about it and throw a great tantrum. What do you do? What do you say? He decidedly refuses to go, getting more and more agitated. How do you resolve this situation?

You manage to get him in there, despite the fact that he is still crying and screams that he doesn't want to go any further. You continue going deeper and deeper into the cavern with this child. Become aware of your feelings, thoughts and sensations.

Suddenly you spot some light rays coming from the end of that subterranean passage. You know that you are coming to the end of it. You also know that you will need to leave the child there at the exit, even though you may not want to. Feel your emotions as you face this dilemma. You must leave him. You must say goodbye. How will you do this? What will you say to him? When the moment comes, what does he say? What is his reaction to your leaving him? What happens to him as you leave him there?

Separating yourself from him... see him in the distance as you continue on your way back through the same paths you covered to get there, except that you don't have to go through the cavern now.

As you pass the body of water you perceive a great luminosity. Upon approaching it you notice that there is a Great Angel there. Looking upon his face you are deeply moved by his eyes which seem to irradiate a deep and loving compassion such as you never saw in human eyes. Observe those eyes, taking in their colouring and the feelings that they evoke in you. Feel what he is saying through that look. Feel his voice inside your heart. Approach him in deep and profound gratitude and allow him to embrace your whole body.

He now offers you a gift. What is it? Take it into your heart so that it stays with you. The Angel wants you to know that he accepts you. He wishes that you be happy. He doesn't want to see you suffer any more. He wants you to be freed from all your burdens, and having seen all that you have gone through, his irradiation now heals and blesses you. He wants you to remain anchored in truth, in deep acknowledgement of the inherent wisdom which is your real nature.

This Angel emanates such a brilliant coloration that he lends you the right measure of courage, clarity and fortitude necessary to liberate you from all burdens and to help you realize this. Breathe in that irradiation and allow it to saturate your cells. Before leaving, he communicates that he will be with you whenever you need him. Tenderly separate yourself from the Angel to make your way back to the point where the star left you and see that it is still there, waiting to take you home.

As you leave the Planet of Truth behind you, you begin to enter into the atmosphere of earth. Notice the deceleration of the vibratory frequency of your body of light, slowly, steadily approaching the building and then the room... sitting back down upon your chair... decelerating deeper and deeper... and bringing back with you all the experience gained in the plane of truth, blending now into your cells. Transfer the impressions or symbols onto your physical body. Remember to feel without identifying with

Whereas the woman needed to keep her focus internally to allow external expressions of the chaos as it surged through her in almost violent waves, he now needs to maintain his clarity of mind while also allowing the profound and shattering softening to occur from within. If both parties can sustain their focus upon the growing consciousness of the heart there is growth.

Most often there are periods of war, or outright cessation. She will try to incite him. Whereas he must stay vulnerable and strong, he may try to sway her with his uncertain fragility. Or he may try to battle with her head on, which is a grave mistake. On the other hand, under the influence of a profound vulnerability, he will feel the urge to lose himself in her, to give in or in some cases to withdraw altogether. Whereas she must stay supportive and separate, she may succumb to her instinct to protect, whereby she loses a husband and gains a son. In this way she annuls her own process and his. Instead of maintaining her positionality with affectionate determination, she may reject him altogether.

Man as much as woman needs support as well as challenge, in order to sustain the growing momentum in the sexual act as in the psychological interplay, in order to integrate with the opposite polarity within. Unless this stage is passed successfully the individual will remain alienated from his potency, which if ignored seeks an irrational modality. This stage of cleansing the temple is like meeting the adversary within. If the couple holds in mind that the conflict is not with the other but rather the inner expression of emerging forces, it can attain to victory.

With the passing of time the ideal couple, liberated through the sexual encounter and the ensuing confrontation, becomes integrated and the opened energies flow through the entire organism, bringing creativity and multiple expressions, transforming the personality and the world of the individual.

But the testing continues. Anything could upset the tenuous harmony achieved and alter the vibrational frequencies attained within the relationship. This corresponds to the second stage or keeping the temple clean. If the state of high-voltage harmony is sustained, at this point the candles of the temple are lighted in the chamber of the heart. But any sudden gust of wind can blow them out. Any foreign, grosser particles can invade the chamber to change the quality of the fire and ignite yet again the lower passions. Harmony must be maintained even more importantly here, without losing intensity or focus. Any moment now the Supreme Guest might appear. The test consists in maintaining the interest without wavering, without boredom or fatigue: the test of fidelity and purpose.

One is also tried in discernment now, learning to differentiate between that which is oneself and that which is another; what belongs to oneself and what is created outside. Tremendous storms will try to distract each partner from the inner reality, attempting to engage the person elsewhere. In some cases individual karma has been largely burnt but the participants may be swayed and deviated from their purpose by outside forces which contaminate the purity of the union by adding excessive and extraneous burdens upon them.

This last period is the waiting. This waiting must be done in the most aesthetic and positive frame of reference possible. Light attracts more light. One day, swiftly, softly, imperceptibly both are lifted into realms of sublime ecstasy. If they again manage to sustain the increased frequencies, they again filter through the entire organism and settle there in a new modality of behaviour which will reflect upon the entire life, atmosphere and surroundings. If integrated properly, more energy, more joy, vitality and clear perception of What Is will be reached.

Yet again... and always... the vigil. As long as we are in a human body... until the inevitable second birth, no longer through the death of the personality's egoism but through that of the very soul which births God Himself within the newly created vehicle of transluscent substance – Consciousness, through the ascended body of Real Man. It will be the Guest, consciousness as Love, who will love through us. The lover and the beloved are, as Sufis say, but two attributes of the essence of Love. They cannot become One unless they return, as in alchemy, to essence.

At that point they may be together or they may be separate, and it will not matter. Extracted from the emotions love emerges like a perfume into all of existence. The principle of love acts through you and me, through everyone... as the one consciousness of Humanity. The expression of God as Love upon the earth culminates in perfect brotherhood.

Individuality and Brotherhood

In Community, Master Morya suggested that the real cooperation or oneness required of a group, can only be achieved when each individual member has reached a level of self-knowledge, equivalent to dominion or mastery. The awareness which emerges is the creative potential and the power to transcend personal interest in favour of the common well-being of the group. This holy purpose has been only too frequently heralded by groups in the past whose good intentions did not quite match the level of mastery over the personal self of its members. The beautiful words of the American Declaration of Independence, where Hierarchy had a strong influence, attest to such good intentions.

On the bandwagon of the New Age, many riders hail a victory which is far from being won. Few people have stopped to consider just what self-knowledge, mastery, transcending personal interest, or even cooperation really mean experientially. The key perhaps lies in the understanding of the term individuality.

Individuality, not personality, is the essential ingredient for friendship, marriage and group relationships. This individuality can only be achieved through the process of consciousness built upon the foundation of the heart as outlined throughout the pages of this book. The process of consciousness is identical in any organization, religion or philosophy. The way into real power is through the softening and testing of the heart. Unless there is a profound sense of who one is both as an essence and as an individual expression of that essence in a grounded flexible personality-structure that is under the direction of consciousness, there is no meeting possible. All that we would see would be projections of ourself.

Without any real meeting, how could there be co-operation? This is what is happening in the world today with its rampant violence and persecution. With hate, fear and obligation weighing upon from the outside and pressuring us from within, it is no wonder that the word 'brotherhood' is thrown about so carelessly.

I was shocked to discover, particularly in South America where I least suspected it, how deeply rooted the hatred is between brothers and sisters, despite the family code being especially strong. Beneath all the veneer of social ethics there is raging selfishness. Perhaps this is a common dynamic which deserves our serious and sustained attention. Unless this phenomenon is confronted and transformed, there is no way in which we will ever make it as a planetary consciousness.

Another important ingredient in groups as in marital relationships and relationships between friends, is a sense of committment. True committment emerges naturally when consciousness is anchored. In that light it appears as a spontaneous and intelligent choice, revealing that committment is to the Self, and that Self includes us all. How can there be a separation if whatever I do to another I am doing to myself vibrationally and tangibly within my very own organic and energetic network? How could I idolize or worship anyone to the exclusion of the rest of humanity, as happens in many relationships between couples and in those relationships between student and teacher?

The truth is that whatever is separated from the whole will pull from a polar opposite counterpart. If I insist in seeing only the beautiful, the ugly will stare me in the face; if I adore an All-Benevolent God, then the devil will chase me even in my dreams. And how could I compete with another one for some imaginary recognition or reward when I am, in the Presence of myself, whole and secure?

Real responsability can only be elicited from individuals. This means neither the cult of personality, whether of the self or projected onto another, nor the selfish alienation which poses as individuality, a syndrome more typical of the northern climates. The non-personal approach to committment is as false and egocentric as the overly-personalized one, which is the trademark of the Latin countries.

The energy of the times dictates groupal work. Individual work is stressed only as a means of attaining to groupal consciousness. If we thought that the power released by two humans in orgasmic union at the level of the heart is great, can we not imagine what unity of purpose and activity can be produced when several individuals are in syntony within the consciousness of the heart? Private relationships and individual satisfaction are not, and never have been the goal. They are simply the intuitings of a greater union, a deeper, fuller experience when a part cooperates in consciousness with the whole in brotherhood.

We would do well to review Alice Bailey's Glamour: A World Problem[13], written almost fifty years ago but painting the precise picture of groupal dynamics in action today, marked by rivalry, disharmony and competition. Most of the traits described there are apparently harmless tendencies but their roots grow upon fertile personalistic trends which germinate as offshoots onto all ambits of human relationship. They are low frequency, culturally accepted norms, which pollute our planetary consciousness as a whole and any attempt at disseminating spiritual teaching.

Group Dynamics and Team Work

In the group category can be included the family unit and the team work behind education, business, finance and spirituality. It is perhaps the most complex form of refining the self, especially in overcoming the illusions which occur among members of a group. If we think that we are finished with the testing in relationships, the groupal experience (or maybe that within your own family) will usually reveal that there is a lot more to learn.

As one enters into a group activity of any duration, there is a mechanism which sets to work creating a group identity. The highs and the lows, the good and the bad all get inextricably welded together at the level of the lower self, unless the individuals maintain their individuality or vertical positioning with the Self. Even if one or several people succeed in sustaining their alignment and high frequencies, if the sum total of the group vibrations or forces are heavier that those, then those too will topple with the rest and sink into the lower frequency range.

The dynamic between the leader of a group and the group itself is especially important. The group happens around a leader or inspiration which is a symbol of the group purpose. If the motivation of the members contain any illusions around devotion, loyalty, idealism or sentimentality, the expectation placed upon the leader will surely be superhuman. With the disillusioment that is bound to occur with people who worship compulsively, it is not suprising that the atmosphere becomes contaminated, weighing heavily upon the other members whose ideals are sincere and appropriate. Add to this the illusion of selfish, righteous responsability on the part of an administration, and you have a genuine viper's nest.

If the leader of the group does not have his two feet firmly rooted in the ground in all senses, or if he is in any way needy of personal human affection, then the illusion of the love-of-being-loved may add to the downfall of the group, particularly in Latin American countries where emotional demonstration is so often a ticket for attention. There are many other variants to this phenomenon. The unconscious projection of the leader himself brings about the contra-projections of the group. The games are especially intricate within the individual regarding himself, the work, the leader, and the other members of the group.

Within a unit or group of people, individuals portray attributes present in varying proportions within each person. In this way you may find different psychological types and structures rather dramatically balancing the equilibrium within a family, which is the classic karmic unit of groupal dynamics. The children play out the unconscious projections of the patriarch or matriarch. The head of the family often represents the inspirations or aspirations of the children and/or other members of the family.

A group can succeed only if the whole unit has the kind of integration corresponding to that which the individual must have within himself upon reaching the level of the heart. In this way the individual represents the model for the family, for the nation, and eventually for the world. In a family this is many times portrayed by separate members, providing physical grounding and ability (usually by dad or big sister), emotional security (which may be dear mother or aunt Tillie), mental development (perhaps by little Harry, the book-worm), and spiritual incentive (by the strange middle sister, or maybe again mother herself). In the past humanity evolved through this dynamic. The growth of the family was synonymous to that of the individual.

Whereas it is extremely important to accept and honour parents (because their dynamics are within you, and any enmity or rejection will reflect back upon yourself), this respect does not represent abdication of the personal power which is the responsibility of the self, or rebelliousness, which is a waste of human resources.

These issues must be settled integrally by the individual before he attains to any true spirituality.

The success of a groupal activity is dependent not only on the degree to which the members are attuned to a common goal but also on the efficiency of the tangible resources available within the group. Both the ideals and the resources of the group must match. This is another way of saying that the ideals must be grounded in practicity. A group usually dissolves for several reasons revolving around three primary elements: (1) The level of practical visionariness of the leader, (2) the level of committment among the members, (3) the amount or kinds of outside or environmental difficulties. The latter are the most difficult to spot and to erradicate as they involve group glamour that is induced by the planetary life and inherent in substance itself.

The rather innocuous tendency of do-gooders within spiritual organizations to improve upon rituals, or to try to 'personally' embellish what is already a good thing, must be curtailed at the onset. Disharmony sets in by such imperceptible emanations of self-righteousness, pride, over-dedication, prickly fastidiousness, obsessional busyness and a myriad other noises of the lower self. The most deadly are the incessant chatter which masks emotional insecurity, the eager sincerity which seeks to pry and dominate, and the unnecessary criticism which pretends to be constructive.

Spiritual team work is still in its infancy. I find that very few such groups attain to their goal, primarily because its members have not yet reached a level of consciousness which can sustain the high voltages that the activity requires. In cases where affirmations and light invocations are used, you will usually find that there is a continual lack of financial resources. This is due to the poor stability and integration at the level of the lower centres of the members. Whereas we do see cases of wealthy 'spiritual' organizations, these are all too often operating on a disguised astral plane and backed by rather sinister forces posing as altruistic humanitarianism.

It is important to understand that everything pertaining to the handling of material forces (sex, money, power, etc) will remain largely in the hands of the dark ones until we as a planetary unit have redeemed that matter and those forces, forming a strong alliance that 'closes the door where evil dwells'. (quote from 'The Great Invocation'.) We must individually conquer that terrain within our own body and in our world, truly embodying the power of light.

Group work must be approached carefully, as humbly and as seriously as any personal relationship, in order to avoid the unconscious distortions which abound everywhere. These unconscious projections will vary from culture to culture but are basically the same mechanism: the personality's egoism conniving to persist.

The group unconscious phenomenon in Brazil stresses emotional family-type manipulation, hiding behind false fear, over-preoccupation with emotional security, an inner personal ambitiousness which is justified by idealistic terminology and devotion. In countries such as the United States and some places in Europe the dynamic is quite different. There the illusion of materialism, or the exaggerated emphasis on form swallows up the vulnerable webs of inspiration at the core, engendering a deadening process that can only produce artificial light. Everywhere the dark side of humanity glaring its ugly face erects pedestals for its idols and still... oh, yes, still crucifies them.

When enough people can sustain the voltages and true insight gained from the vertical alignment and centring within the heart, we will attain to true brotherhood upon the Earth. Then the vestal virgins will not only keep the fire, they will burn as flames themselves within the fire of consciousness and real spirituality.

In the same proportion and to the same extent that we blossom in our relationship to ourselves, to our partners, family and friends, we are each contributing to the brotherhood of Man. In this way each relationship is a sacred trust which leads to the highest form of sacrifical love, that of serving the Greater Self of Man.

The human alchemical experience begins with toddler steps through every act and ends everywhere, stretching out into Infinity and embracing the Great and Glorious Mighty 'I AM'.

Published in Great Britain by
ASHGROVE PUBLISHING
an imprint of
HOLLYDATA PUBLISHERS LTD
55 Richmond Avenue
London N1 0LX

© 2002 Zulma Reyo

ISBN 1-85398-142-7

First Edition

Revised and abridged edition of
'KARMA AND SEXUALITY: The Human Alchemical Experience',
published in Spanish and Portuguese translation in 1992 by
Kier (Buenos Aires, Argentina) and Ground Publishers (Sao Paulo, Brasil).

The right of Zulma Reyo to be identified as the author of
this work has been asserted by her in accordance with the
Copyright Designs and Patent Act 1988.

All rights reserved

No part of this publication may be reproduced, stored in a
retrieval system or transmitted, in any form or by any means,
electronic, mechanical, photocopying, recording or otherwise,
without the prior permission of the publisher.

Book Design by Brad Thompson
Cover Illustration by Diane Barker
Printed and bound in Malta by Interprint

NOTES

1 pg 10 Karma: Sanskrit term meaning cause and effect.

2 pg 11 Bio physical energy and vitality are used interchangeably in this text conveying the idea of a basic energy which ignites human experience. This energy includes sexuality but does not limit itself to sexual behaviour.

3 pg 14 'atman': An Eastern term meaning 'primary unit'. The word 'atom' was derived from it.

4 pg 35 These concepts about energy and force, including the correlation between sub-atomic activity and the human dynamic were passed on to me by Sandra Galeotti. The insights gained by her came after years of study in the fields of nuclear physics, esoteric science and Jungian psychology and form the central core of her thesis developed in courses and presented in manuals. The information triggered such an exciting revelation in me that it came to form an integral part of the work within Inner Alchemy. For the full version of these ideas, the reader is referred to the book, Esoterism and Self Knowledge by Sandra Galeotti, published in Portuguese. (Ed. Ground).

5 pg 52 Correlates express an energy at a higher octave of frequency in a healthy, integrated progression, but also distortedly express the rejected or repressed characteristics of the lower centres in a more powerful frequency

6 pg 62 The entry for 'possession' however, occurs through lower centres, including the nape and temples. Through those openings collective subconscious thoughtforms seek to influence undiscerning humanity.

7 pg 102 Arthur Janov, founder of The Primal Institute and author of 'The Primal Scream', Putnam.

8 pg 122 Sufism: a Middle Eastern school of thought founded on the esoteric teachings of the Koran.

9 pg 125 See pps. 281-282, 'Mastery: The Path of Inner Alchemy', Janus.

10 pg 129 This segment can be extended to include a contemplation of the chakras from within, gently directing your awareness to them in order to balance them. You may use your hands, positioned in both the front and back section of the body to re-centre them.

11 pg 130 In more advanced practices, the students of Inner Alchemy use the figure of light (another of Olive Pixley's exercises) as an earthing in light. See Inner Alchemy, page 100.

12 pg 145 As you may remember, this nerve is governed by the heart chakra.

13 pg 171 In the English language version, pages 120-123 contain an accurate list of some of the commonly held 'glamours' operating through people of different personality characteristics.